Printing-Process Control and Standardization

Printing-Process Control and Standardization

Robert Y. Chung

RIT Press
Rochester, New York

Published and distributed by:
RIT Press
90 Lomb Memorial Drive
Rochester, New York 14623
http://ritpress.rit.edu

ISBN 978-1-939125-74-3 (print)
ISBN 97810939125-75-0 (e-book)

Printed in the U.S.A.
Book and cover design: Marnie Soom

Library of Congress Cataloging-in-Publication Data

Names: Chung, Robert, author.
Title: Printing-process control and standardization / Robert Y. Chung.
Description: Rochester, New York : RIT Press, 2020. | Includes
   bibliographical references and index. | Summary: "In Printing-Process
   Control and Standardization, Robert Chung explains the process of color
   printing with relevant examples related to measurement, process-control,
   color management, and standardization. Chung provides detailed
   information for teaching students in print media or graphic
   communication, as well as for seasoned industry professionals"—
   Provided by publisher.
Identifiers: LCCN 2020020864 (print) | LCCN 2020020865 (ebook) | ISBN
   9781939125743 (softcover) | ISBN 9781939125750 (ebook)
Subjects: LCSH: Color printing. | Color printing—Standards. | Color
   printing—Textbooks. | Printing industry—Standards. | Process control.
Classification: LCC Z258 .C496 2020 (print) | LCC Z258 (ebook) | DDC
   686.2/3042—dc23
LC record available at https://lccn.loc.gov/2020020864
LC ebook record available at https://lccn.loc.gov/2020020865

Dedication

The author wishes to dedicate this book to Milton Pearson, former principal imaging scientist at RIT Research Corporation, Rochester, New York. Milt was the author's academic mentor and thesis advisor at RIT School of Printing in 1975. Milt was an avid jogger. He kept a log and was fond of saying, "If the sample size is one, you learn nothing about variation." His passion for color, imaging, data collection, and the scientific approach to problem-solving influenced the author immensely.

Contents

Foreword

I became acquainted with Robert (Bob) Chung at the Rochester Institute of Technology in Rochester, New York, while he was teaching several classes and I was teaching a number of seminars. Later on, we both became involved with the Technical Association of the Graphic Arts (TAGA), where Bob presented several papers and guided many students with their publications, which were presented at TAGA conferences, later appearing in *TAGA Proceedings*, a scholarly journal. Bob had a profound and positive influence on those students. He was there with a helping hand and a gently guiding voice. Bob's relationship with the technologists and scientists who were also members of TAGA was one of mutual respect and politeness. Bob is well respected by his peers. He was the 2006 recipient of the Michael H. Bruno TAGA Award for Outstanding Contribution to the Graphic Arts Industry.

This book is written for students as well as for the printing professionals and other graphic communication specialists to help them better understand process control and standardization, with a strong emphasis on control. Control and standardization are two very difficult goals to achieve, especially when they relate to color. The late George Jorgenson of the Graphic Arts Technical Foundation said that "there are 125 variables on an offset press that have to be controlled." Couple that observation with paper variations, ink variations, customer requirements, and viewing conditions, and it becomes evident that printing is not an easy process to control.

In the early 1970s, the need for standardization and process control was driven primarily by the magazine publishing industry. The same advertisement printed in three different magazines in different plants looked quite different. Thus, the renewed interest in standards and control developed. The body of knowledge from the 1970s to the present has grown substantially due to the efforts of many industry professionals and organizations.

In *Printing-Process Control and Standardization*, I call your attention to the clarity of writing and the ability of the author, Bob Chung, to place the technology in proper perspective. Bob guides the reader to the standards and measurements that work well for printing, as opposed to standards for paint, fabric, and textile industries. Many of the figures in the book bring clarity to understanding color variation, for example, the figure showing different RGB working space was quite interesting. Color should not be a "moving target," but one that is always under control.

With regard to standards, the time and effort that the international community has devoted to this effort has been outstanding. This book clearly describes the various standards and their relevance to the graphic communications industry. Standards are not the least common denominator in printing, but a target to be obtained to satisfy customer needs. They will change over time as needed along with the changes in technology.

As a final thought, it is often said that we are measured by what we leave on this earth. Hopefully, this book will teach and inform not only students, but those who work within the industry.

The TAGA papers that Bob Chung has written contribute to our knowledge. But perhaps his most important legacy is his influence as a good teacher by helping his students contribute to this body of knowledge.

Thank you, Bob, for your book and knowledgeable contributions to the printing industry.

Raymond J. Prince
Former VP of National Association for
Printing Leadership
Former Director of Technical Services for
Printing Industries of America

Preface

This book covers color measurement, printing standardization, and their applications in printing-process control and printing-conformity assessment. The goal is to provide a textbook for college curricula to address the science and technology of process color printing. In addition to students, prepress technicians, production specialists, and technically curious professionals in the graphic arts industry will also find the book useful.

The author taught the contents of this book at Rochester Institute of Technology School of Media Sciences for more than 36 years. In the 1980s, students were taught printing technologies using image carriers (plates/cylinders). Pictorial color reproduction, printed using offset lithography and flexography, is termed "analog printing" in this book. Today, the graphic arts industry has been transformed into the graphic manufacturing industry. Pictorial color images are captured, edited, verified, exchanged, and printed digitally. Pictorial color reproduction printed using inkjet or electrophotography without fixed image carriers is termed "digital printing" in this book. All these changes in printing technology gave the author the opportunity to emphasize the fundamentals, and tell the story of technological pushes and customer demand pulls in the graphic communication industry.

One might argue that standardization suppresses creativity and stifles innovation. As an expert in ISO/TC 130 and the convenor of the Working Group 13 on printing conformity assessment from 2010 to 2015, the author would argue that standardization can help maximize compatibility, safety, and quality. By addressing common needs and articulating feasible solutions, standardization defines product specifications that are accepted in the market. Standardization, in turn, allows products or services to be created in the most cost-effective manner, making them more attractive to consumers and promoting economic growth.

There are nine chapters in this book. Chapter 1 covers densitometry, where process control metrics, for example, solid ink density and tonal value increase, are introduced. Chapter 2 covers colorimetry, and colorimetric metrics, for example, CIELAB, and ΔE, are introduced. Tristimulus integration, metamerism, and chromatic adaptation are also explained. Chapter 3 provides an overview of ICC color-management system, that is, how we manage pictorial color images as data that computers understand. Chapter 4 discusses printing standardization and introduces some notable ISO/TC 130 printing standards. Chapter 5 introduces printing conformity assessment, certification scheme guidelines, and certification activities around the world. Chapter 6 examines press calibration methods applicable to analog and digital printing processes. Chapter 7 discusses printing-process control for analog and digital printing. Chapter 8 describes *Test Targets*, an RIT publication and a collection of case studies about printing technology, process control, and color management. Chapter 9 addresses the changing nature of the printing industry by highlighting new printing standards development and revisions of existing standards to meet print buyers' needs.

The book was printed using a four-color digital press on coated paper. Adobe Creative Suites (Photoshop, Illustrator, InDesign) were used in the design and printing of the book. Many illustrations in this book describe visual differences as a result of different software, hardware, and consumable settings, for example, using one printing condition to simulate visual differences of many printing conditions, and using one printing condition to simulate visual differences of printing variations within a pressrun. Thus, it was important for the author, the book designer, and the printer to share the same color management settings throughout the color reproduction workflow.

The contents of this book have been taught successfully to students of widely varying educational preparation. Laboratory exercises are outside the scope of the book. A brief summary with multiple-choice questions and essay-type questions is included at the end of each chapter to ensure comprehension of the material.

The author wishes to thank Franz Sigg, former faculty member at the RIT School of Media Sciences, for his collaboration and support in the past four decades. A special thank-you goes to Lingjun Kong, Shanghai Publishing and Printing College, for encouraging the author to write this textbook.

Robert Y. Chung
Professor Emeritus of School of Media Sciences
Rochester Institute of Technology
Rochester, New York

1 Densitometry

This chapter covers how a densitometer works. It also covers density-derived values and densitometry applications, including pressrun analysis. After reading this chapter, one should know that a densitometer measures light absorption due to the presence of colorants, such as ink and toner. Being sensitive to differences in dark shades, a densitometer is good at measuring colorant amounts, which makes it an ideal tool for printing-process control.

1.1. Densitometer Fundamentals

A densitometer is an electronic instrument consisting of a light source, a measurement aperture, color filters, a light-sensitive detector, and associated circuitry to display density and density-derived values. There are two types of densitometer used in the printing industry: reflection and transmission densitometers.

1.2. Reflection Densitometer

A reflection densitometer is used to measure press sheets printed using CMYK (cyan, magenta, yellow, and black) inks. Figure 1.1 is a schematic of a reflection densitometer. The geometry of the light source and the light-sensitive detector (or photocell) is 45/0, meaning the light source is directed at a 45° angle in a conical manner to the sample, and the diffuse reflectance is measured at a 0° angle, or vice versa. There are four filters (red, green, blue, and visual) in the optical path to provide four filter densities for every measurement. As shown in Figure 1.1, a cyan ink film is measured; the highest density (red filter density), displayed as "C 1.35," is an indication of the cyan ink film thickness. This is the main reason why a reflection densitometer is used for process control in the pressroom. Other filter densities of the cyan ink are less meaningful from the process control point of view.

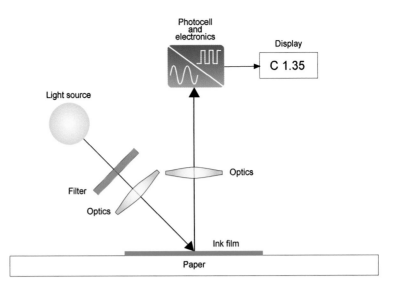

Figure 1.1.
Schematic of a
reflection densitometer.

As shown in Eq. 1.1, reflection density (D_R) is defined as the logarithm (base 10) of the reciprocal of the reflectance (R) of a sample. If we know the density of a sample, we can calculate its reflectance using Eq. 1.2.

$$D_R = \log_{10} \frac{1}{R} \qquad\qquad \text{Eq. 1.1}$$

$$R = 10^{-D_R} \qquad\qquad \text{Eq. 1.2}$$

Table 1.1 shows the relationship between visual sensation, reflectance, and density of a gray scale. If we express sample reflectance (column 2) in the form of scientific notation (column 3), then the density of the sample (column 4) is the exponent without the negative sign. To elaborate, a perfect white patch reflects all incident light, it has a density of 0. A light gray patch reflects one-half of the incident light, it has a density of 0.3. In other words, the logarithmic difference of 0.3 is a difference of 2 in real numbers.

Table 1.1. The relationship among visual sensation, reflectance, and density.

Visual sensation	Reflectance	Scientific notation	Density
Perfect white	1.0	1×10^0	0
Light gray	0.5	$1 \times 10^{-0.3}$	0.3
Gray	0.25	$1 \times 10^{-0.6}$	0.6
Dark gray	0.1	1×10^{-1}	1.0
Black	0.01	1×10^{-2}	2.0

The Richter scale is used to measure the severity of an earthquake. Being a logarithmic number, an increment of "1" has a difference of "10" in real numbers. Density is also logarithmic. A density range of 3.0 represents a 1000:1 difference between light and dark in an outdoor scene. When the outdoor scene is photographed and reproduced on a coated paper, the light-and-dark ratio of the scene is compressed to 100:1 or a density range of 2.0. If the outdoor scene is printed on newsprint, the light-and-dark ratio of the scene is further compressed to 10:1 or a density range of 1.0.

Before being used, the densitometer must be calibrated using a specified white patch and a black patch. The process of calibration typically requires the white patch measurement only. This is because the black patch measurement can be carried out by the instrument without human intervention.

When density measurements are made relative to the reference white patch, this is known as the absolute density. When measurements are made relative to the paper density, this is known as the relative density. Printing standards use absolute density to specify solid ink density aim points. For printing-process control, relative densities are used to indicate ink film thickness, where a density of "0" means there is no ink on the paper. Relative densities are also used to generate a 1-D transfer curve, discussed in chapter 6, "Device Calibration."

1.3. Transmission Densitometer

A transmission densitometer is used to measure density and dot area on high-contrast graphic arts films. Figure 1.2 is a schematic of a transmission densitometer. The light source and the photocell are situated on either side of the object. The film is the object, shown in side view as well as in top view.

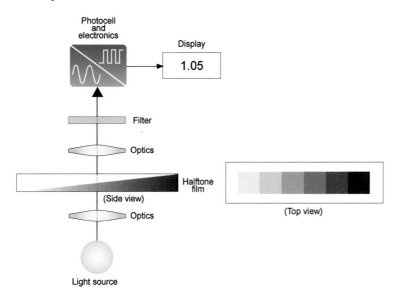

Figure 1.2.
Schematic of a transmission densitometer.

There is no color filter in a graphic arts transmission densitometer. This is because all measurements are limited to black-and-white photographic films. However, special filters may be used to assess how films respond in orthochromatic (blue- and green-sensitive films) or UV-sensitive film environments.

As shown in Eq. 1.3, transmission density (D_T) is the log of the reciprocal of the transmittance (T) of the sample. If we know the transmission density of a sample, we can calculate its transmittance using Eq. 1.4.

$$D_T = \log_{10} \frac{1}{T}$$
Eq. 1.3

$$T = 10^{-D_T}$$
Eq. 1.4

In film-based printing workflows, transmission densitometers are calibrated without a film in place of the optical path. When measuring the maximum density (Dmax) of lithographic (lith) films, the transmission density often goes to 6 or more. This means only one part in a million (1×10^6), or nearly no light, can pass through a developed lith film base. A lith film not only has high maximum density, but also high contrast. This gives sharp edges when reproducing type. It also gives sharp edges around halftone dots on film.

1.4. % Film Dot Area (%FDA)

In film-based halftone photography, a transmission densitometer is also a dot area meter. When a halftone film is measured, the dots are the part of the film that does not transmit light. Equation 1.5 describes the conversion from transmission density to % film dot area (%FDA) when measuring halftone film with a transmission densitometer.

$$\%\text{FDA} = (1 - T) \times 100$$
$$= (1 - 10^{-D_T}) \times 100$$

Eq. 1.5

On the other hand, Eq. 1.6 describes the conversion from % film dot area to transmission density, .

$$D_T = \log_{10} \frac{1}{\left[\frac{100 - \%\text{FDA}}{100}\right]}$$

Eq. 1.6

If we plot transmission density (D_T) as a function of % film dot area (Figure 1.3), the relationship is logarithmic, that is, the minimum film density (Dmin) is at 0% FDA, 0.3 film density is at 50% FDA, and 2.0 film density is at 99% FDA. The maximum film density (Dmax) of greater than 3.0 is close to the solid tone or 100% FDA.

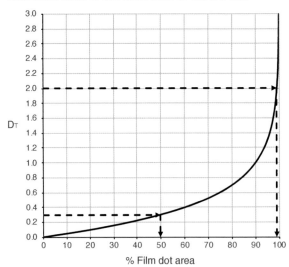

Figure 1.3.

Transmission density (D_T) as a function of % film dot area.

This means that the change between highlight dots (5%–10%), as explained in Eq. 1.7, corresponds to a small change in transmission density (0.03), and the change between shadow dots (90%–95%), as explained in Eq. 1.8, corresponds to much larger changes in transmission densities (0.30).

Printing-Process Control and Standardization

$$\Delta D_T = \log_{10} \frac{1}{\left[\frac{100-10}{100}\right]} - \log_{10} \frac{1}{\left[\frac{100-5}{100}\right]} = 0.05 - 0.02 = 0.03 \quad \text{Eq. 1.7}$$

$$\Delta D_T = \log_{10} \frac{1}{\left[\frac{100-95}{100}\right]} - \log_{10} \frac{1}{\left[\frac{100-90}{100}\right]} = 1.30 - 1.00 = 0.30 \quad \text{Eq. 1.8}$$

1.5. Filter Transmittance

Four (red, green, blue, and amber) filters are used in a reflection densi-tometer. Figure 1.4 shows spectral transmittance of these gelatin Wratten filters, per Kodak Photographic Filters Handbook (Eastman Kodak, 1990).

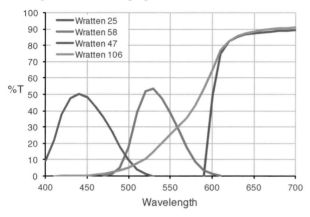

Figure 1.4.
Spectral transmit-tance of color filters in a reflection densi-tometer.

To explain, the visible spectrum ranges from 400 nm to 700 nm. The blue filter (Wratten 47) transmits the lower one-third of the energy (400–500 nm) of the visible spectrum. The green filter (Wratten 58) transmits the middle one-third of the energy (500–600 nm) of the visible spectrum. The red filter (Wratten 25) transmits the upper one-third of the energy (600–700 nm) of the visible spectrum. These filters, also known as wide-band filters, are suitable for color separation work and for measuring cyan, magenta, and yellow ink film thicknesses in process color printing.

The amber filter (Wratten 106), which transmits more long-wave-length energy than short- and medium-wavelength energy, is suitable for converting photocell response in a densitometer to the luminosity response of the eye. As such, the Wratten 106 filter is used for measuring the black ink film thickness in printing.

1.6. Reflectance and Density of Process Inks

Theoretically, cyan, magenta, and yellow inks completely reflect two-thirds of the energy from the visible spectrum and completely absorb one-third of the energy from the visible spectrum. In reality, the cyan ink reflects its own hues, that is, the blue and green portions, and absorbs that of complementary hues, or long-wavelength energy (Figure 1.5). When the cyan solid is measured through a red filter, the low red reflectance turns into a high red-filter density. Thus, the red-filter den-sity is the desired density indicating the cyan ink film thickness.

The magenta ink reflects the blue and red portions of the visible spec-trum and absorbs medium-wavelength energy (Figure 1.6). When the magenta solid is measured through a green filter, the low green reflec-tance turns into a high green-filter density. Thus, the green-filter density is the desired density indicating the magenta ink film thickness.

By the same token, the yellow ink reflects the green and red portions

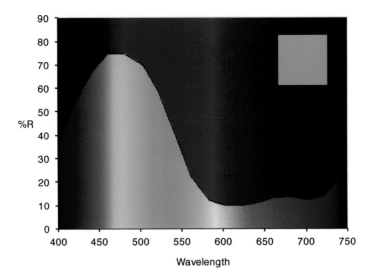

Figure 1.5.
Spectral reflectance and absorption of the cyan ink.

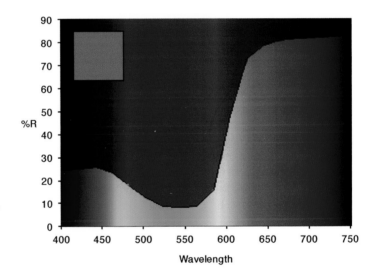

Figure 1.6.
Spectral reflectance and absorption of the magenta ink.

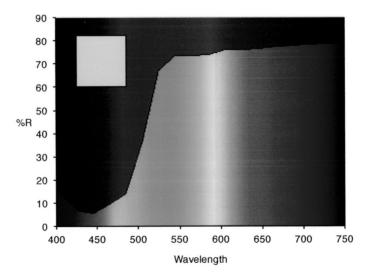

Figure 1.7.
Spectral reflectance and absorption of the yellow ink.

Printing-Process Control and Standardization

of the visible spectrum and absorbs short-wavelength energy (Figure 1.7). When the yellow solid is measured through a blue filter, the low blue reflectance turns into a high blue-filter density. Thus, the blue-filter density is the desired density indicating the yellow ink film thickness.

1.7. Density Increment and Visual Sensation

If we examine a gray scale visually, for example, Kodak Control Scale R-14, with equal density-increment between adjacent steps from highlight to shadow (Figure 1.8), the density difference in the light region of the gray scale will be perceived as having a larger visual difference than the same density difference in the shadow region of the gray scale. A benefit of describing visual sensation as density is that it is specific and can be documented. Density, when defined as numbers, differentiates dark shades more than the human eye can. This is why density is an effective process control tool to control ink film thickness during printing.

Figure 1.8.
A gray scale with equal density increments between adjacent steps.

1.8. Wide-Band Densitometer

The spectral responses of a wide-band (Status T) densitometer, specifying the source–filter–detector combination, are indicated by the solid (red, green, and blue) lines in Figure 1.9. Status T has been adopted by the North American printing industry. The 0/45 geometry and the use of the black opaque backing for density measurement have also become standardized.

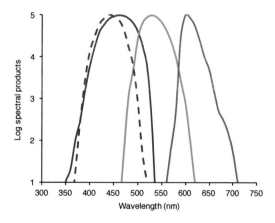

Figure 1.9.
Source–filter–detector combination of Status T (solid lines) and Status E (dotted lines) responses.

1.9. Narrow-Band Densitometer

Narrow-band (Status E density) densitometers, widely adopted in Europe, use a blue filter that passes less than 100 nm of energy in the short wavelength of the visible spectrum (dotted blue line in Figure 1.9). In other words, Status E density produces the same red-filter density of cyan ink and the same green-filter density of magenta ink, but a higher blue-filter density (e.g., 1.3) than Status T density (e.g., 1.0) when measuring a yellow solid ink patch.

There are two advantages with a narrow-band (Status E) densitometer. First, it has a higher response to yellow ink film variations, and thus is suitable for process control in the pressroom. Second, narrow-band densitometers have better interinstrument agreement than wide-band densitometers.

1.10. Density Dry-Back

The geometry of 45° illumination and 0° pick-up, or vice versa, is standard in reflection densitometry. In other words, the diffuse component of the reflected beam is measured, and the specular component is ignored. Figure 1.10 illustrates the difference between the specular reflection (left) and the diffuse reflection (right) of an ink film. To explain, when light is reflected from a freshly inked surface, as illustrated in Figure 1.10 (left), there is less diffuse or scattered component, detected by the photocell, thus, producing higher density. As illustrated in Figure 1.10 (right), there is more diffuse or scattered component of the reflected beam as the ink film dries. Thus, dry ink film produces lower density. The difference between the wet ink density and the dry ink density, for example, 0.05 less density, is known as density dry-back.

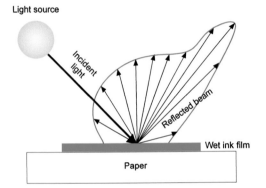

Figure 1.10.
Specular reflection (left) and diffuse reflection (right).

Printing aim points are specified as dry ink density. If conformance to printing standards is of the essence, the solution for process control in the pressroom, where wet ink density measurement cannot be avoided (e.g., in sheetfed offset printing), is to examine the density dry-back and adjust the wet density aims to account for the density dry-back.

1.11. Unpolarized and Polarized Density

Polarizing filters are used in sunglasses to reduce glare from the sun. They are also used in photography to make white clouds stand out more from the blue sky. But how does polarization work? What's the effect of polarization in densitometry?

A polarizing filter passes the light parallel to the filter's polarization axis and blocks light polarized at 90° to the filter's polarization axis. Sunglasses made from polarizing filters can effectively block light like a visor. When scattered light from the blue sky is blocked by a polarizing filter in front of the lens, more contrast is rendered between a white cloud and the blue sky. Polarization filters placed in the optical path of a densitometer minimize the first surface reflection. Thus, polarized density eliminates the difference between wet ink and dry ink density readings, making density dry-back a nonissue.

1.12. Densitometer and Anomalous Trichromat

A densitometer is useful in measuring and controlling solid ink density or ink film thickness during press makeready and printing. It is a step in the right direction toward achieving quality printing. But there are many factors that affect print quality, for example, sharpness, visual defects, and so on, that a densitometer cannot measure.

A densitometer provides filter densities through red, green, and blue filters. Although it has trichromatic responses, a densitometer is an "anomalous trichromat." It does not measure color, only colorant amount.

1.13. Film-based and Computer-to-Plate Workflows

In a film-based printing workflow, densitometers are used to characterize the input–output relationships between original density and film dot area, film dot area and plate dot area, and plate dot area and print density. Figure 1.11 presents photomicrographs of halftone dots on a film negative (left), on a plate (center), and on a print (right).

In a CTP (computer-to-plate) workflow, densitometers are used to

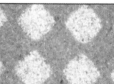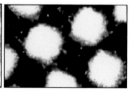

Figure 1.11.
Photomicrographs of film negative dots (left), plate dots (center), and printed dots (right).

characterize the input–output relationship between % digital dot and printed dot. In either case, densitometers are used to provide density data for printing-process control.

1.14. Density-derived Metrics

Densitometry played an important role in transitioning graphic arts to being a manufacturing industry. Other than using solid ink density to control the color gamut of process inks, a number of density-derived metrics were developed to characterize ink–paper–press interactions. These metrics are TVI (tonal value increase, or dot gain), print contrast, ink trapping, and midtone spread.

1.15. %TVI, % Dot Gain, or the Murray-Davies Equation

TVI is the darkening of the halftone tints as the inked dots are transferred from a plate to paper. This darkening is caused by the spread of the inked dots at the printing nip (physical dot gain). It is also caused by light penetrating the unprinted paper, being trapped by ink dots, and never exiting the paper (optical dot gain).

The %TVI is defined as the increase between % film (or digital) dot and % print dot. Two researchers, Alexander Murray and E.R. Davies, developed the TVI (dot gain) formula (Eqs. 1.9 and 1.10), based on density measurements (Murray, 1936). When %TVI is communicated as a single value, the dot size defaults to 50% FDA or 50% digital values.

$$\%TVI = \% \text{Dot}_{Print} - \% \text{Dot}_{Film\,(Digital)} \qquad \text{Eq. 1.9}$$

The % paper dot is calculated using Eq. 1.10. Dt, Dp, and Ds denote tint density, paper density, and solid density, respectively. Furthermore, these densities are complementary filter densities of the process inks, that is, RC (red-filter density of cyan ink), BY (blue-filter density of yellow ink), and GM (green-filter density of magenta ink).

$$\% \, \mathrm{Dot_{Print}} = \frac{1 - 10^{-(Dt-Dp)}}{1 - 10^{-(Ds-Dp)}} \times 100 \qquad \text{Eq. 1.10}$$

The % film dot is measured by a transmission densitometer (Eq. 1.11). In a CTP workflow, plate dots are defined by digital values or measured by a plate video analyzer.

$$\% \, \mathrm{Dot_{Film}} = \left[1 - 10^{-(Dt-Dp)}\right] \times 100 \qquad \text{Eq. 1.11}$$

Notice that the difference between Eqs. 1.10 and 1.11 is the denominator. This is because the maximum density of a lith film (~6.0) is so high that the denominator, is literally unity or 1.

Figure 1.12 is an example of a film dot area target, called CMYK step wedges, with known % dot area values and screen rulings. It is suitable for constructing the plate/press curve and the TVI (or dot gain) curve upon printing, measurement, and graphing.

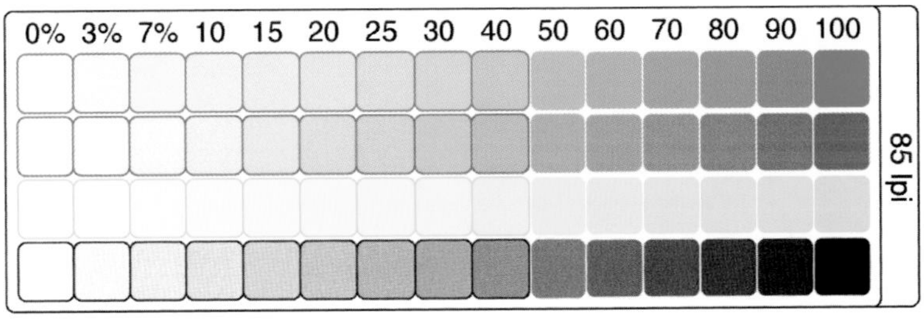

Figure 1.12.
A step wedge with known % dot area. (Image courtesy of Franz Sigg.)

To explain, Figure 1.13 (left) is an example of the plate/press curve, with print density as the *y*-axis and % dot area as the *x*-axis. It emphasizes solid ink densities of CMYK inks. Using the same data, Figure 1.13 (right) is the TVI curve with %TVI as the *y*-axis and % dot area as the *x*-axis. TVI values are zero at 0% and 100% dot area. The TVI curve emphasizes the highlight-to-midtone contrast.

Figure 1.13.
Print density vs. % dot area (left); TVI vs. % dot area (right).

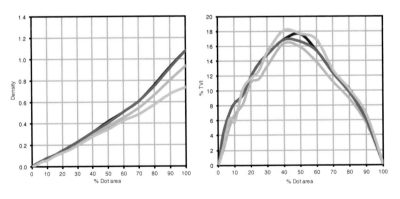

Printing-Process Control and Standardization

1.16. % Print Contrast (%PC)

While the %TVI is computed by using relative density to emphasize the highlight-to-midtone contrast, % print contrast (%PC) is computed by using absolute density to emphasize the shadow contrast. In Eq. 1.12, D_{75} is the density of the 75% dot area and D_s is the density of the solid.

$$\%PC = \left[\frac{Ds - D75}{Ds}\right] \times 100 \qquad \text{Eq. 1.12}$$

1.17. % Apparent Ink Trap

In lithographic four-color printing, the common ink lay down sequence is cyan (first), magenta (second), and yellow (third), with black either first or last. When printing two chromatic inks together, for example, magenta ink on top of the cyan ink, % ink trap is used to measure and monitor the overprint color. What is % ink trap?

The % ink trap is a measure of how well the second ink is transferred (or trapped) on top of the first ink relative to its coverage of an unprinted substrate. Figure 1.14 illustrates a top view and a side view of printing a magenta ink film on top of a cyan ink. D1 is the density of the first (cyan) ink on an unprinted substrate; D2 is the density of the second (magenta) ink on an unprinted substrate; and D3 is the density of the overprint (blue). All three densities are measured with the complementary filter of the second ink layer.

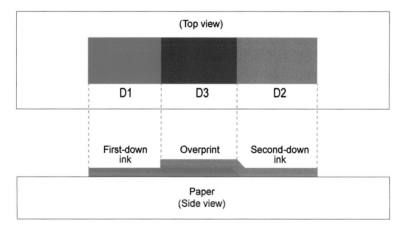

Figure 1.14.
A schematic of an ink trap.

A number of ink trap formulas have been proposed. The most commonly used ink trap formula, Eq. 1.13, was developed by Frank Preucil in 1958 (Field, 1985).

$$\% \text{ Apparent ink trap} = \frac{D3 - D1}{D2} \times 100 \qquad \text{Eq. 1.13}$$

If we examine Eq. 1.13 mathematically, we can see that when % Apparent ink trap is 100%, the sum of the individual densities, (D1 + D2), is equal to the density of the overprint, D3. But additivity of density does not hold in process color printing (Yule, 1967). To avoid possible misunderstanding that the formula has physical significance, Preucil called this equation the "apparent ink trap." In other words, Eq. 1.13 does not estimate the physical ink trap amount. But when the apparent ink trap changes during printing, we can ascertained that the overprint colors are affected.

1.18. Midtone Spread (MTS)

ISO 12647-1 (ISO, 2012b) defines midtone spread (MTS) using Eq. 1.14, where Ax is measured tonal vale, Axo is specified aim points, and x is c, m, or y (for cyan, magenta, or yellow). MTS impacts gray balance due to dot gain deviations among cyan, magenta, and yellow printing conditions.

$$\text{MTS} = \text{Max}\left[(A_c - A_{co}), (A_m - A_{mo}), (A_y - A_{yo})\right] - \qquad \text{Eq. 1.14}$$
$$\text{Min}\left[(A_c - A_{co}), (A_m - A_{mo}), (A_y - A_{yo})\right]$$

1.19. Process Ink Evaluation

ISO 2846-1 (ISO, 2006) standardizes how we assess the color of the process inks. Before ISO 2846 was developed, densitometers were used to assess the color of process inks. Such assessment is based on the assumption of "ideal" inks. An ideal process ink completely absorbs one-third of the visible spectrum (high desired density) and completely reflects the other two-thirds of the visible spectrum (zero desired density).

When measuring real ink patches, desired densities are not high enough, and unwanted densities are nonzero. Nevertheless, desired density (D_H) is higher than the two unwanted densities, which are denoted as medium (D_M) and low (D_L) densities. Based on the high, medium, and low values of the three filter densities, Frank Preucil of GATF developed the following three formulas, Eqs. 1.15–1.17, for process ink evaluation (Field, 2004).

$$\% \text{ Hue error} = \left(\frac{D_M - D_L}{D_H - D_L}\right) \times 100 \qquad \text{Eq. 1.15}$$

$$\% \text{ Efficiency} = \left(1 - \frac{D_M + D_L}{2 \times D_H}\right) \times 100 \qquad \text{Eq. 1.16}$$

$$\% \text{ Grayness} = \frac{D_L}{D_H} \times 100 \qquad \text{Eq. 1.17}$$

In comparison to the ideal ink, hue error of the process ink is caused by the medium density (D_M); grayness (or dirtiness) of the ink is caused by the low density (D_L); and the two unwanted densities $(D_M$ and $D_L)$ and the desired density (D_H) are responsible for the efficiency of the ink.

1.20. Density- and TVI-based Printing Standards

ISO 12647-2 (ISO, 2013b) is an international printing standard that uses TVI values to specify printing aim points and tolerances. In general, higher paper grade produces higher solid ink density (SID) with lower TVI values. Detailed discussion on printing standards, including some notable international printing standards, is covered in chapter 4, "Printing Standardization."

1.21. Densitometer Features and Benefits

Densitometers used to be stand-alone instruments. This is not the case anymore, because most color-measurement instruments are capable of measuring color spectrally. Status T density and CIELAB (pronounced "C-lab") values are computed on the fly and displayed according to the user's needs.

A handheld densitometer is suitable for manual operations and laboratory use. As shown in Figure 1.15, an X-Rite i1 Pro2 is a spectro-densitometer with a scanning attachment and can be used to measure a color proof.

Figure 1.15.
A handheld spectro-densitometer, i1 Pro2. (Published with permission from X-Rite Inc.)

An off-line scanning densitometer, shown in Figure 1.16, is suitable for color measurement in a production environment. Pressroom personnel can verify not only inking uniformity across all ink zones, but also inking consistency during the pressrun.

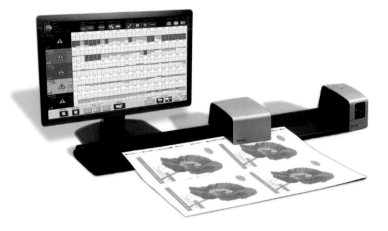

Figure 1.16.
An off-line scanning spectro-densitometer, IntelliTrax2. (Published with permission from X-Rite Inc.)

Table 1.2. Press sheet analysis summary.

Solid ink density	Yellow	Magenta	Cyan	Red	Green	Blue	Black	White
Visual filter (K)	0.04	0.52	0.52	0.53	0.57	1.07	1.08	0
Red filter (C)	0.01	0.16	0.94	0.16	0.93	0.98	1.07	0
Green filter (M)	0.07	1.08	0.27	1.09	0.33	1.04	1.09	0
Blue filter (Y)	0.74	0.59	0.10	1.12	0.75	0.55	1.09	0

Density at 75% FDA	Yellow	Magenta	Cyan	Red	Green	Blue	Black	White
Visual filter (K)	0.04	0.40	0.39				0.69	0
Red filter (C)	0.01	0.13	0.61				0.69	0
Green filter (M)	0.07	0.68	0.21				0.69	0
Blue filter (Y)	0.54	0.43	0.08				0.68	0

Density at 50% FDA	Yellow	Magenta	Cyan	Red	Green	Blue	Black	White
Visual filter (K)	0.02	0.27	0.26				0.42	0
Red filter (C)	0.01	0.09	0.38				0.42	0
Green filter (M)	0.04	0.41	0.14				0.42	0
Blue filter (Y)	0.35	0.27	0.05				0.41	0

Calculations	Yellow	Magenta	Cyan	Red	Green	Blue	Black	White
% Dot gain	18	17	16				18	
% Print contrast	28	37	35				37	
% Ink trapping				72	88	71		
% Hue error	8	47	20	97	70	88		
% Grayness	1	15	11	14	35	53		
% Efficiency	95	65	80	44	42	26		
Midtone spread		7						

1.22. Densitometric Applications

We can use a handheld densitometer to perform a press-sheet analysis. This includes tone reproduction (% dot area vs. solid ink density and % dot area vs. %TVI), and print contrast, and ink trap of red, green, and blue overprints. Table 1.2 is a summary of these metrics when analyzing process color printing for quality assurance.

We can use a scanning densitometer to conduct the spatial uniformity analysis by measuring solid ink densities across all ink zones from a press sheet. This is a press makeready activity and is influenced by ink consumption of the print form. Figure 1.17 illustrates the uniformity of the magenta solid across the width of a press sheet. The *y*-axis is the density difference from the mean, and the *x*-axis is the ink zone across the width of the press.

Figure 1.17.
Spatial uniformity of magenta solid ink density.

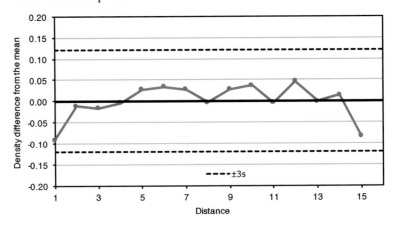

We can also use a scanning densitometer to analyze the temporal consistency in a pressrun, that is, stability of solid ink densities and %TVI over time (from the beginning to the end of a pressrun). Figure 1.18 illustrates the black solid ink density variation over time with the aim point, upper spec, and lower spec limits superimposed.

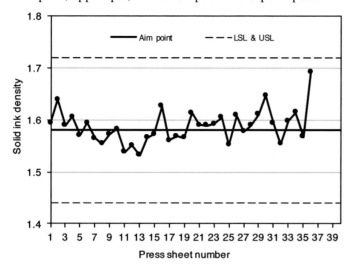

Figure 1.18.
Black solid ink density over time.

Press personnel are familiar with controlling ink film thicknesses based on densitometer readings. chapter 7, "Printing-Process Control," provides detailed discussions on how to apply Beer's law to adjust solid ink density to achieve colorimetric conformance of solid ink coloration.

1.23. Chapter Summary

A densitometer measures light absorption due to the presence of a colorant, such as ink or toner. It can quantify and differentiate dark shades better than the human eye can. This is the reason that densitometers are useful for process control in four-color printing.

A printing workflow is about putting dots on film or a plate and putting ink on paper. In the beginning, it was accomplished by skilled and experienced craftspeople. Today, the graphic arts industry is a part of the manufacturing industry in which ink, paper, platemaking, and printing have been standardized. Densitometry has been instrumental in the transformation of printing from a crafts-based industry to a manufacturing-based industry.

1.24. Multiple-Choice and Essay Questions

1. In process color printing, _____ has the biggest impact on the size of the process ink color gamut.
A. solid ink density
B. dot gain
C. print contrast
D. hue error

2. The major difference in calculating % film dot and % paper dot is that _____.
A. Dmax of film is too low
B. Dmin of film is too high
C. solid ink density is not high enough
D. paper density is not low enough

3. For ink trap calculations, all three filter densities are measured with the complementary filter of the _____ ink layer.
A. first-down
B. second-down
C. overprint
D. All of the above

4. A density difference of _____ between two adjacent steps in a gray scale suggests that the reflectance ratio between the two steps is 2 to 1.
A. 2.0
B. 1.0
C. 0.6
D. 0.3

5. The fact that _____ makes densitometers useful process control tools in press work.
A. density and visual sensation are linearly correlated
B. densitometers are sensitive to differences in light shades
C. densitometers are sensitive to differences in dark shades
D. All of the above

6. There is a positive correlation between density and light _____ of a sample.
A. transmission
B. refraction
C. reflection
D. absorption

7. Reflection densitometers are used to analyze _____ attributes such as dot gain and print contrast. They can also be used to evaluate _____ attributes such as hue error and grayness.
A. separation film, press sheet
B. press sheet, process ink
C. process ink, paper
D. paper, separation film

8. Which expression correctly describes the % film dot area?
A. (1 – transmittance) × 100
B. % transmittance
C. (1 – density) × 100
D. (1 – opacity) × 100

9. Given that press sheet 1 has a solid ink density of 1.00, and press sheet 2 has a solid ink density of 1.15, what is the reflectance factor between the two solid ink patches?
A. 2
B. square root of 2
C. 0.15
D. 0.5

10. A densitometer is an anomalous trichromat. This is because _____.
A. it measures light absorption
B. it does not model normal human visual responses
C. it has a narrow band response
D. it is not influenced by the surroundings

11. Why is a densitometer useful for process control in four-color printing?

12. What is TVI? How does TVI relate to physical dot gain and optical dot gain?

2 Colorimetry

Colorimetry has surpassed densitometry as the metrology of choice for specifying tone and color requirements in the graphic arts industry. After reading this chapter, one should know the basics of color vision, how the CIE (International Committee on Illumination) specifies color by numbers, and CIEXYZ-derived color space models. This chapter also describes color matching, color difference, and the concepts of device-independent color.

2.1.   Light, Object, and Color Vision

Light exists as a form of energy and can be measured in terms of wavelength. When an object is illuminated by a light source, a portion of the light is absorbed by the object and a portion of the light is reflected. When the reflected light reaches the human eye and is interpreted by the brain, the visual sensation is called color. In other words, visual sensation requires the presence of light, an object, and an observer (Figure 2.1).

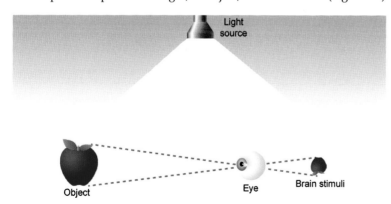

Figure 2.1.
Interaction among light, an object, and an observer.

2.2.   How the Eye Works

When a picture is taken with a film-based camera, the lens allows light to transmit and focus on the film. When the light exposes the film, a photograph is taken. Today, CCD (charge-coupled device) sensors in the digital camera replace silver inhalide emulsion used in film-based cameras.

The eye works in the same way as a camera. The front part of the eye, including the cornea, pupil, and lens, allows light to pass through. The back inside wall of the eye is called the retina. The retina is like the film or CCD sensors of the camera. The light reaches the center of the retina, called the fovea, which has three types of sensors (red-sensitive cones, green-sensitive cones, and blue-sensitive cones). In daylight, we rely on the fovea to see details and color. The light also reaches to the periphery of the retina, called rods. At night, we rely on the periphery of the retina to see the general shape of things and detect movements.

2.3. Organizing Color

Imagine a sailor was trapped on a deserted island, surrounded by pebbles of all colors. To keep his sanity, the sailor decided to rearrange the pebbles from their random order into a visual order. He proceeded to sort pebbles with different color names (hues) like red, green, and blue, into separate piles. He recognized that the leftover pile had no distinct hue (i.e., achromatic), but varied from white to light gray to dark gray to black (lightness). When he examined the red pile more closely, he could further separate the pebbles into bluish-red, red, and yellowish-red piles. By sorting other colored piles, he discovered the opponent color pairs of red–green and yellow–blue that described hue-to-hue relationships. Finally, he was able to organize pebbles of the same hue with varying lightness (value) and colorfulness (chroma).

This story illustrates the work of Albert H. Munsell (1858–1918), an American art teacher and the inventor of the Munsell color system (Luke, 1996). Figure 2.2 shows that color has three dimensions: hue, value (lightness), and chroma and can be organized in a three-dimensional space.

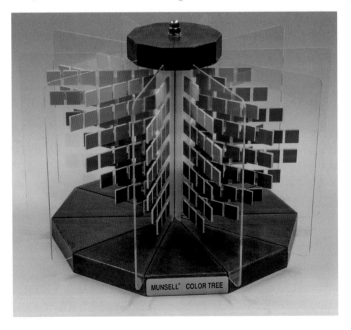

Figure 2.2.
Munsell color tree. (Retrieved with permission from Hannes Grobe, https://commons.wikimedia.org/wiki.)

2.4. Observer Variation

Assuming that lighting and an object are fixed, color may be perceived differently by different people. This is because color perception is influenced by biological differences among observers.

How do we know that biological differences contribute to variation in color vision? We can test the observers using the Ishihara's test for color blindness. Notice that the term "color blindness" means "abnormal color vision" in people who see color distorted. The test uses randomized color dots, having similar chroma, but different hues to differentiate between figure and ground. Color-normal individuals may recognize the figure as a number, where color-deficient individuals would not. As shown in Figure 2.3, a color-normal individual sees the number 3 as a green figure against the red and orange background. But an individual with red–green deficiencies sees the test plate differently (Ishihara, 1962).

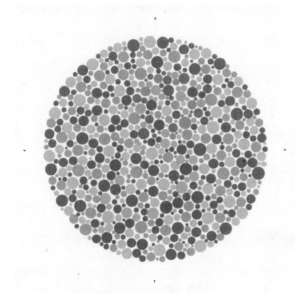

Figure 2.3.
An Ishihara test plate for color blindness. (Retrieved with permission from the Science Museum, London, https://commons.wikimedia.org/wiki.)

We can also tell that biological differences contribute to variation in color vision by using the Farnsworth-Munsell 100 hue test. The test includes four wooden cases. Each case consists of 21 color caps that are removable and two fixed caps, situated at either end of the case (Figure 2.4).

Figure 2.4.
Farnsworth-Munsell 100 hue test. (Published with permission from X-Rite Inc.)

Standard lighting should be used when administering the color vision test. Before being presented to the observer, the removable caps should have been randomized. The objective of the test is to arrange the caps according to hue. The observer is asked to find the cap which looks most like the fixed cap and place it there and repeat the process for the rest of the movable caps.

Each of the 84 removable caps is numbered on the reverse. The test is scored by examining the number. If there are four or fewer two-cap transpositions, the observer's color discrimination is rated superior. An average normal observer will have up to seven two-cap transpositions.

Observers with defective color vision, also known as anomalous trichromats, have a midpoint between 50 and 70 transpositions. Statistics indicate that 7% of the male population and less than 0.5% of the female population are anomalous trichromats (Birch, 2001).

To specify color by numbers, CIE, which is the international authority on light and color, developed a standard based on how normal observers see color.

2.5. 1931 CIE 2° Standard Observer

This section describes the relationship between the sensitivity of the human eye and the wavelength of light. W. D. Wright and J. Guild carried out their color-matching experiments independently using 17 color-normal individuals (Hunt, 1987). As shown in Figure 2.5, the observer sees a small disk with two half-fields. The control side of the half-field is illuminated by a selected wavelength of the visible spectrum. The experimental side of the half-field is adjustable by three (red, green, and blue) light sources. The experiments were designed to quantify how spectrum colors are matched. When the two half-fields are matched, the observer would see a uniform disk. The color-matching experiments were repeated by selecting a different wavelength until the entire visible spectrum was sampled.

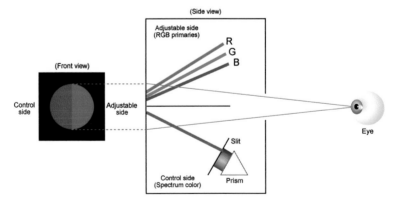

Figure 2.5.
Schematic of the color-matching experiment.

Initial results of the color-matching functions showed three weaknesses: (1) negative values, as the result of moving the lights from the experimental side to the control side in order to make the match; (2) lack of information concerning the amount of light; and (3) an unequal area under the three color-matching functions.

To overcome these three weaknesses, higher-order mathematics was used to transform the data based on the three light sources (real primaries) into three imaginary primaries such that (1) there was no negative value; (2) the lightness function was the same as the green-sensitivity function; and (3) all three color-matching functions had the same area under the curve, thus assuring that equal stimulus values would produce neutral sensations. This is the CIE 1931 2° standard observer or the color-matching functions that specify the amounts of primaries needed to match the monochromatic test color at a specified wavelength (Figure 2.6).

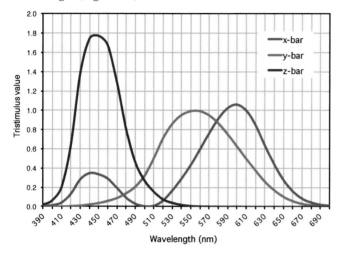

Figure 2.6.
CIE 1931 2° standard observer.

2.6. 1964 CIE 10° Supplementary Observer

Color vision is mainly centered around 2° from the fovea, where cones are heavily concentrated. Foveal vision is suitable for graphic arts applications. However, a CIE 10° standard observer was established in 1964 to accommodate industrial color matching in larger visual fields such as large flat labels, rigid packages, paints, textiles, and plastic applications.

2.7. Spectral Power Distribution and CIE Illuminants

Now, we turn our attention to the quantification of the light source. Light exists as a form of energy and can be measured by a spectro-radiometer. Figure 2.7 shows the spectral power distribution (P) of CIE illuminant A. This is the tungsten light commonly used in households. It emits more long-wavelength energy than short-wavelength energy and has a color temperature of 3200 kelvins (K).

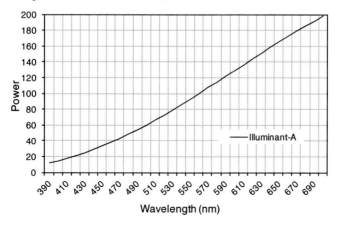

Figure 2.7.
Spectral power distribution of illuminant A.

Figure 2.8 shows the spectral power distribution of CIE illuminant D50. This is the standard illuminant used in graphic arts viewing booths. D50 means daylight with a color temperature, the hue of the light source, of 5000 K. As the color temperature goes higher, the hue of the light source becomes bluer.

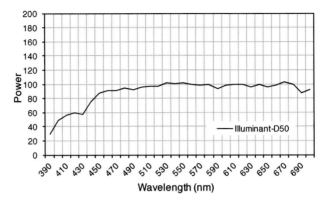

In addition to spectral power distribution and color temperature, the CRI (color-rendering index) is a measure of how continuous (i.e., lacking "spikes" of energy) spectral energies are across the visible spectrum. It describes the color-rendering capability of a light source.

2.8.   Object Reflectance

An object modifies the energy of a light source by means of absorption and reflection. A spectrophotometer is used to measure the spectral reflectance (R) of a sample across the visible spectrum. Figure 2.9 shows the spectral reflectance of a Pantone 165 coated (C) solid as a function of the wavelength (λ). Designers and print buyers pay attention to the high saturation of the orange color. Press operators pay attention to the ink film thickness of the spot color ink or whether the color can be matched using the standard CMYK process inks.

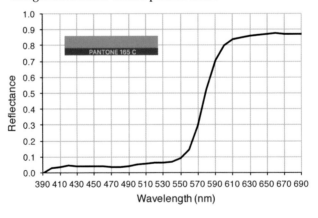

2.9.   Tristimulus Integration

As mentioned earlier, it is the reflected light that reaches to the human eye. The color sensation, as quantified, is called the tristimulus values (X, Y, Z). Tristimulus value is the integration of the light source (P), object reflectance (R), and color-matching functions of the CIE standard observer. Figure 2.10 is a graphic depiction of the tristimulus integration.

Printing-Process Control and Standardization

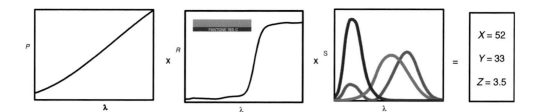

Equations 2.1–2.4 are used to calculate tristimulus values mathematically. The computation may take place automatically within a spectrophotometer or can be generated using an Excel spreadsheet.

Figure 2.10.
A graphic depiction of tristimulus integration.

$$X = k \sum_{400}^{700} P_{(\lambda)} R_{(\lambda)} x_{(\lambda)}$$ Eq. 2.1

$$Y = k \sum_{400}^{700} P_{(\lambda)} R_{(\lambda)} y_{(\lambda)}$$ Eq. 2.2

$$Z = k \sum_{400}^{700} P_{(\lambda)} R_{(\lambda)} z_{(\lambda)}$$ Eq. 2.3

$$k = \frac{100}{\sum P_{(\lambda)} y_{(\lambda)}}$$ Eq. 2.4

D50 and the CIE 2° observer have been become standards in the graphic arts industry. Thus, they become the weighting factors, $W_x(\lambda)$, $W_y(\lambda)$, and $W_z(\lambda)$ of spectral reflectance, $R(\lambda)$, where λ goes from 400 nm to 700 nm. Equation 2.5 shows how the red stimulus (X) is integrated, Eq. 2.6 shows how the green stimulus (Y) is integrated, and Eq. 2.7 shows how the blue stimulus (Z) is integrated.

$$X = \sum_{400}^{700} R(\lambda) \times W_X(\lambda)$$ Eq. 2.5

$$Y = \sum_{400}^{700} R(\lambda) \times W_Y(\lambda)$$ Eq. 2.6

$$Z = \sum_{400}^{700} R(\lambda) \times W_Z(\lambda)$$ Eq. 2.7

$W_x(\lambda)$ is the weighting factor at λ for tristimulus value X. $W_y(\lambda)$ is the weighting factor at λ for tristimulus value Y. $W_z(\lambda)$ is the weighting factor at λ for tristimulus value Z. These equations have been programmed in spreadsheets and commercial software and hardware.

By means of tristimulus integration, colors can be expressed using their tristimulus values, that is, the amount of red stimulus (X, pronounced "cap-x"), green tristimulus (Y, pronounced "cap-y"), and blue tristimulus (Z, pronounced "cap-z") seen by the standard observer.

When analyzing a printed color control strip in the XYZ color space, keep in mind that the higher the tristimulus values are, the lighter or more colorful the color is. As shown in Table 2.1, paper white (C0M0Y0K0), printed with no tonal value, has the highest tristimulus values (78.4X, 81.2Y, 64.9Z) of all patches. The gray patch (C50M40Y40), printed with moderate amounts of cyan, magenta, and yellow tonal value, has a tristimulus values of 3.3X, 24.0Y, 20.2Z. The 3C solid patch (C100M100Y100), printed with full amount of 3-color tonal value, has a tristimulus values of 3.6X, 3.7Y, 3.0Z.

Table 2.1. Relationship between tonal values and tristimulus values.

ID	C	M	Y	K	X	Y	Z
Paper	0	0	0	0	78.4	81.2	64.9
Gray	50	40	40	0	23.3	24.0	20.2
3C solid	100	100	100	0	3.6	3.7	3.0
K100	0	0	0	100	2.6	2.6	2.0
C100	100	0	0	0	14.0	21.1	44.8
M100	0	100	0	0	34.2	17.7	14.9
Y100	0	0	100	0	64.7	69.0	7.3

The cyan printer is a red-light absorber. The tristimulus values of the C100 patch are (14.0X, 21.1Y, 44.8Z), indicating that the cap-X (14.0X) of the cyan color is the smallest of the three stimuli. The magenta printer is a green-light absorber. The tristimulus values of the M100 patch are (34.2X, 17.7Y, 14.9Z), indicating that the cap-Y (17.7Y) of the magenta color is smaller, but not the smallest, due to the unwanted absorption of the magenta ink in the short-wavelength region. The yellow printer is a blue-light absorber. The tristimulus values of the Y100 patch are (64.7X, 69.0Y, 7.3Z), indicating that the cap-Z (7.3Z) of the yellow color is the smallest of the three stimuli. Nevertheless, the interpretation of color in the CIEXYZ space is not intuitive.

2.10. XYZ-derived Color Spaces

Two XYZ-derived color spaces are introduced in this chapter. The first is the 1931 CIEYxy color space. Next is the 1976 CIELAB color space.

CIE also adopted the chromaticity coordinates, Yxy, in 1931. Y is the lightness of the color; x (pronounced "little-x"), expressed in Eq. 2.8, represents fractional redness; y (pronounced "little-y"), expressed in Eq. 2.9, represents fractional greenness; and z or (1-x-y) is the fractional blueness.

$$x = \frac{X}{X+Y+Z} \qquad\qquad \text{Eq. 2.8}$$

$$y = \frac{Y}{X+Y+Z} \qquad\qquad \text{Eq. 2.9}$$

Chromaticity coordinates, x and y, have been used to illustrate the horseshoe-shaped locus where all colors of the spectrum lie in relation to the imaginary primaries (Figure 2.11). The illuminant lies in the middle of the chromaticity diagram. For example, illuminant D50 has a chromaticity coordinate of (0.34x, 0.35y).

A color can be specified graphically in the chromaticity coordinates, xy, with the addition of two more parameters: (1) the dominant wavelength is the intersection of the line between the illuminant and the color and the spectrum locus; and (2) the excitation purity is the ratio between the distance between the illuminant and the color, divided by the distance between the illuminant and the dominant wavelength. In other words, Y is the lightness, dominant wavelength is the hue, and excitation purity is the chroma of the color, X (Figure 2.12).

When analyzing color by numbers or graphically, a basic assumption is that the analysis should mimic how we see color and judge color differences. To test the assumption as a hypothesis, David MacAdam conducted a series of color-matching experiments. He asked a single

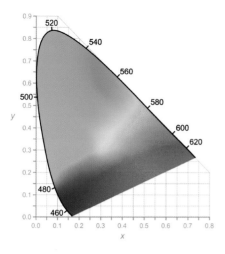
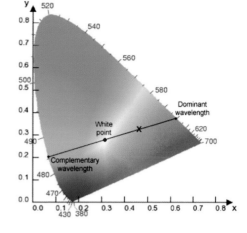

Figure 2.11. Chromaticity diagram. (Retrieved with permission from Peter Hermes Furian, https://www.dreamstime.com.)

Figure 2.12. Dominant wavelength and excitation purity. (Retrieved with permission from https://en.wikipedia.org/wiki/Dominant_wavelength#/media.)

observer to pick colors having equal color differences in relation to a reference color using a visual colorimeter. The body of data that he collected was the uncertainty with which a match of colored lights could be made (Berns, 2000). The experimental findings showed that equal color differences are not graphed as circles of equal sizes, but ellipses of unequal sizes at various orientations. As shown in Figure 2.13, the MacAdam ellipse is an indication that the CIEXYZ or CIEYxy color space is not visually uniform.

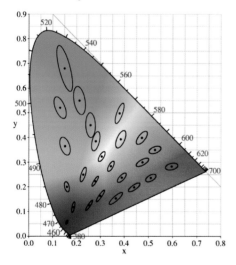

Figure 2.13. MacAdam ellipses. (Retrieved with permission from Wiley-Interscience, https://en.wikipedia.org/wiki/MacAdam_ellipse#/media.)

2.11. 1976 CIELAB Color Space

Starting in 1931, many uniform color space models were proposed by the scientific color community. None were agreed upon until the development of the CIELAB color space in 1976.

Equations 2.10–2.12 illustrate the transformation from CIEXYZ to CIELAB, in which the tristimulus values of the color (X, Y, and Z) and the tristimulus values of the illuminant (X_n, Y_n, and Z_n) are applied. The function, f, is a cube-root equation.

$$L* = 116\left[f\left(\frac{Y}{Y_n}\right)\right] - 16 \qquad \text{Eq. 2.10}$$

$$a* = 500\left[f\left(\frac{X}{X_n}\right) - f\left(\frac{Y}{Y_n}\right)\right] \qquad \text{Eq. 2.11}$$

$$b* = 200\left[f\left(\frac{Y}{Y_n}\right) - f\left(\frac{Z}{Z_n}\right)\right] \qquad \text{Eq. 2.12}$$

The CIELAB color space is based on the opponent color theory: when the brain interprets a color, for example, red, the sensation cannot be interpreted as its opponent, green, at the same time. This is also true for the yellow–blue opponent pair. Thus, a color can be described as yellowish-red, reddish-blue, bluish-green, and greenish-yellow, but not greenish-red or yellowish-blue.

As shown in Figure 2.14, CIE-L* is lightness, CIE-a* is either redness or greenness (it is redness if $a*$ is positive, and greenness if $a*$ is negative), and CIE-b* is either yellowness or blueness (it's yellowness if $b*$ is positive, and blueness if $b*$ is negative). If $a*$ and $b*$ go to zero, the color is neutral.

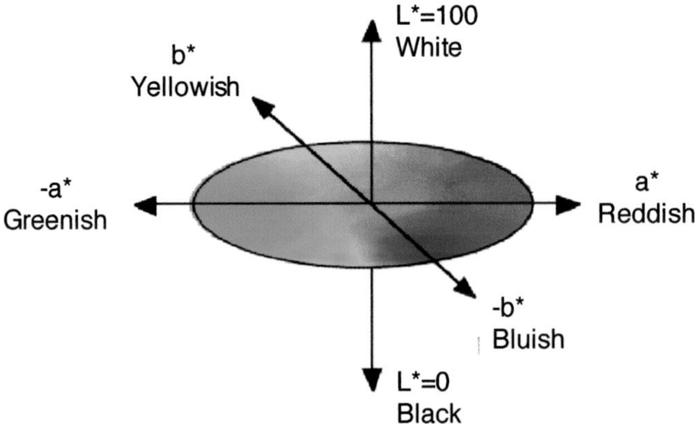

Figure 2.14.
The 1976 CIELAB color space. (Retrieved with permission from Carl K. Anderson, https://www.fhwa.dot.gov/publications/research/safety/13018/002.cfm.)

Table 2.2 is an extension of Table 2.1 with the addition of the CIELAB values for each of the seven colors. Paper white (C0M0Y0K0) has the highest lightness value (92.2$L*$, 0.2$a*$, 2.0$b*$) of all patches. The gray patch (C50M40Y40) has a medium lightness value and small $a*$ and $b*$ values (56.1$L*$,0.7$a*$, −0.7$b*$). The 3C solid patch (C100M100Y100) has a low value (22.7$L*$, 0.0$a*$, 0.4$b*$). The $a*$ and $b*$ values of 3C solid are also near zero.

Table 2.2. Relationship between tonal values and CIELAB values.

ID	C	M	Y	K	X	Y	Z	L*	a*	b*
Paper	0	0	0	0	78.4	81.2	64.9	92.2	0.2	2.0
Gray	50	40	40	0	23.3	24.0	20.2	56.1	0.7	-0.7
3C solid	100	100	100	0	3.6	3.7	3.0	22.7	0.0	0.4
K100	0	0	0	100	2.6	2.6	2.0	18.5	0.5	1.6
C100	100	0	0	0	14.0	21.1	44.8	53.1	-35.2	-44.0
M100	0	100	0	0	34.2	17.7	14.9	49.2	73.1	-0.8
Y100	0	0	100	0	64.7	69.0	7.3	86.5	-4.2	87.7

The C100 patch is a bluish-green color (53.1$L*$, −35.2$a*$, −44.0$b*$), and the $a*$ and $b*$ values are both negative. M100 patch is a reddish-blue color (49.2$L*$, 73.1$a*$, −0.8$b*$), and the $a*$ value is positive, and the $b*$ value is near zero. Y100 patch is a yellowish color (86.5$L*$, −4.2$a*$, 87.7$b*$), and the $a*$ value is near zero, and the $b*$ value is positive.

2.12. 1976 CIELCh Color Space, C^*, ΔC^*, and ΔC_h^*

The vector equivalent of the CIELAB color space is the CIELCh color space (Figure 2.15). Here, L^* is lightness, and metric chroma, C^*, is the colorfulness (Eq. 2.13). ΔC^* is the chroma difference between two colors (Eq. 2.14). Hue angle, h, is the hue angle in radians (Eq. 2.15). The conversion from radian to degree is shown in Eq. 2.16.

$$C* = \sqrt{a*^2 + b*^2} \qquad \text{Eq. 2.13}$$

$$\Delta C^* = C_1^* - C_2^* \qquad \text{Eq. 2.14}$$

$$h_{\text{Radian}} = \tan^{-1}\left(\frac{b*}{a*}\right) \qquad \text{Eq. 2.15}$$

$$h_{\text{Degree}} = h_{\text{Radian}} \times \frac{180}{\pi} \qquad \text{Eq. 2.16}$$

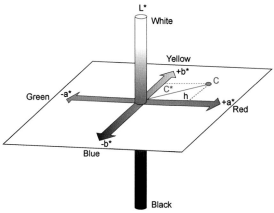

Figure 2.15.
The 1976 CIELCh color space.

Chromaticness difference (ΔC_h), expressed in Eq. 2.17, is the difference between the reference chroma (a^*_1 and b^*_1) and the measured chroma (a^*_2 and b^*_2) of a gray balance control patch, for example, C50M40Y40 (ISO, 2012a).

$$\Delta C_h = \sqrt{\Delta a*^2 + \Delta b*^2} \qquad \text{Eq. 2.17}$$

$$\Delta a* = a*_1 - a*_2 \qquad \text{Eq. 2.18}$$

$$\Delta b* = b*_1 - b*_2 \qquad \text{Eq. 2.19}$$

2.13. XYZ-based TVI

TVI used to be derived using densities per the Murray-Davies equation. When solid colorations of process inks are specified by colorimetry, ISO/TS 10128 (2009) also specifies TVI of CMYK, per colorimetric Eqs. 2.20–2.22.

$$\text{TVI}_{\text{M\&K}} = 100\left[\frac{Y_p - Y_t}{Y_p - Y_s}\right] - \text{TV}_{\text{Input}} \qquad \text{Eq. 2.20}$$

$$\text{TVI}_Y = 100\left[\frac{Z_p - Z_t}{Z_p - Z_s}\right] - \text{TV}_{\text{Input}} \qquad \text{Eq. 2.21}$$

$$\text{TVI}_C = 100\left[\frac{(X_p - 0.55Z_p) - (X_t - 0.55Z_t)}{(X_p - 0.55Z_p) - (X_s - 0.55Z_s)}\right] - \text{TV}_{\text{Input}} \qquad \text{Eq. 2.22}$$

2.14 Spectral Match and Metameric Match

In the textile industry, color matching is in terms of spectral or invariant match. This means that a reference color and a sample color have the same spectral reflectance curves (SRC) and they have the same tristimulus values. The match is independent of light source. Other examples of spectral match include original paints in the automobile industry and automobile touch-up paints sold in auto parts store, yarns for knitting, and household paints.

In the printing, photography, and television industries, a practical approach to color image reproduction is colorimetric match, and not spectral match. This means that color matching often is in the form of metameric (or conditional) match. Metamerism means that $(XYZ)_1$ = $(XYZ)_2$, but $(SRC)_1 \neq (SRC)_2$, where XYZ is the tristimulus value of the two objects and SRC is the spectral reflectance curve of the two objects.

There are two types of metamerism: illuminant metamerism and observer metamerism.

1.   If two objects match under one illuminant, and by changing the illuminant, the pair of objects no longer match, then the pairs are said to exhibit illuminant metamerism. Illuminant metamerism, an interaction between light and color, is about "making two colors look like one" due to tristimulus integration. The RHEM color pair (Figure 2.16), a band-aid-size sticker coated by two dissimilar colorants, is an example of illuminant metamerism, that is, stripes are seen (e.g., $\Delta E > 3$) when light is not 5000 K.

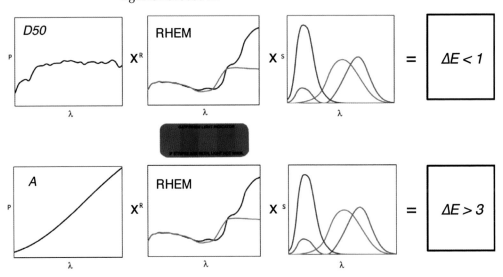

Figure 2.16.
Conditional match of the RHEM metamers.

2.   If two objects match, and by changing the observer, the pair of objects no longer match, then the pairs are said to exhibit observer metamerism. As shown in Figure 2.17, the blue of the morning glory flower and the blue sky match to the human eye (left), but mismatch when photographed (right). The mismatch is due to the fact that the camera's spectral sensitivity goes beyond that of the human eye and into the infrared region (Milton Pearson, private communication by email, March 23, 2013).

Figure 2.17.
An example of observer metamerism (simulated).

2.15. Color Difference, ΔE^*_{ab}

The 1976 ΔE^*_{ab} defines the color difference as the straight line between two colors, C_1 and C_2, in space (Eq. 2.23).

$$\Delta E *_{ab} = \sqrt{(L *_1 - L *_2)^2 + (a *_1 - a *_2)^2 + (b *_1 - b *_2)^2} \quad \text{Eq. 2.23}$$

ΔE^*_{ab} has only magnitude without direction. When we know the ΔE^*_{ab} between C_1 and C_2, and the ΔE^*_{ab} between C_2 and C_3, we know nothing about the ΔE^*_{ab} between C_1 and C_3, unless we know the CIELAB values of all three colors.

2.16. Hue Difference, ΔH^*, and Hue Angle Difference, Δh

Hue difference, ΔH^*, is the residual (leftover) quantity after subtracting ΔL^* and ΔC^* from ΔE^*_{ab} (Eq. 2.24). It is different from the hue angle difference, Δh (Eq. 2.25).

$$\Delta H *= \sqrt{\Delta E *_{ab}^2 - \Delta L *^2 - \Delta C *^2} \qquad \text{Eq. 2.24}$$

$$\Delta h = |h_1 - h_2| \qquad \text{Eq. 2.25}$$

2.17. Color Difference, ΔE_{00}

Colors with equal visual differences (e.g., Munsell colors) were used to assess the degree of color uniformity among various color space models. The 1976 CIELAB color space showed improvement over the 1931 CIEYxy color space. However, the CIELAB-derived ΔE^*_{ab} does not correlate well with visual perception in high-chroma regions. Instead of changing the XYZ-derived CIELAB color space, a new color difference metric, ΔE_{00}, was introduced to overcome the deficiency.

The computational procedure for ΔE_{00} is quite complex, involving the installation of a macro in a spreadsheet. Alternatively, ΔE_{00} may be computed using commercially available software such as ColorThink Pro, X-Rite i1 Pro 2, among others.

2.18. ΔE_{00} versus ΔE^*_{ab}

There are a number of color difference formulas developed by the color science community. A "better" color difference formula implies a more accurate prediction of how the human eye sees color differences. To answer the question, "Is ΔE_{00} a better color difference yardstick than

ΔE^*_{ab}," we can (1) reproduce color pairs in different hues, but with similar color differences in ΔE^*_{ab}, (2) measure and record their ΔE^*_{ab} and ΔE_{00} values, or (3) select observers with normal color vision and visually rank these color differences under standard viewing conditions.

Table 2.3 is an example of ΔE^*_{ab} and ΔE_{00} values collected from such an experiment. If observer visual rankings are inconsistent, we can conclude that ΔE^*_{ab} is a better yardstick, because these colors were prepared to have similar ΔE^*_{ab} values. If, however, observer visual rankings are consistent and are in line with the ΔE_{00} magnitude, that is, the gray pair is consistently ranked the highest, followed by the blue pair, and so on, then we have reason to conclude that ΔE_{00} is a better color difference yardstick than ΔE^*_{ab}.

Table 2.3. Color difference between the color pairs in ΔE^*_{ab} and ΔE_{00}.

Color pair	ΔE^*_{ab}	ΔE_{00}
Gray	5.5	7.9
Red	5.4	2.6
Blue	5.6	5.1
Green	3.9	2.0
Yellow	4.1	2.4

2.19. Index of Metamerism

Two samples having identical tristimulus values for a given reference illuminant or reference observer are metameric if their SRCs differ within the visible spectrum. The index of metamerism is the tristimulus mismatch, expressed by a color difference equation. If the metameric pair do not have identical tristimulus values for the reference condition, the index of metamerism is in error. This is because the index of metamerism assumes that the metameric pair have identical tristimulus values for the reference condition, that is, ΔE is zero for the reference condition. This is usually not the case for real metamers.

The concept of index of metamerism is relevant to graphic arts applications, especially packaging graphics. This is because printed specimens are likely reproduced by different printing (specially formulated or process color) inks, viewed under different illuminants in retail stores (e.g., D50, fluorescent, and tungsten). In addition, printed specimens are viewed by undefined (normal and color-deficient) observers. In such cases, the smaller the index of metamerism is, the better the color match with different observers and illuminants.

2.20. Mean Color Difference from the Mean

Precision is the closeness of randomly selected sample measurements. As shown in Eq. 2.26, precision of a color-measurement process can be described by the mean color difference from the mean (MCDM), that is, the average ΔE between sample CIELAB values and their average CIELAB value.

$$\text{MCDM} = \frac{\sum_{i=1}^{n} \Delta E(\text{Lab}_{\text{Ave}} - \text{Lab}_i)}{n} \qquad \text{Eq. 2.26}$$

MCDM is a measure of precision, repeatability, or reproducibility. The repeatability of a color-measurement process is a measure of precision when carried out by the same person using the same instrument over time. The reproducibility of a color-measurement process is a measure of precision when carried out by different persons using different instruments over time.

Interinstrument agreement affects the reproducibility of a color-measurement process. If one instrument is used to calibrate the press, and another instrument is used to assess the color conformity, we need to know the reproducibility of a color-measurement process in relation to the variation tolerance.

2.21. Frequency, Cumulative Relative Frequency (CRF), and Percentile ΔE

In Figure 2.18, a total of 1617 color patches are specified in the reference printing condition and measured in the sample printing condition. Figure 2.18 (left) is a frequency distribution (or histogram) of ΔE_{00} in seven subgroups. Figure 2.18 (right) is the CRF (cumulative relative frequency) of ΔE_{00}.

"Percentile ΔE" (i.e., ΔE^{*}_{ab} or ΔE_{00}) is an XY plot with the x-axis being the sorted ΔE value, and the y-axis being the CRF value (0–1.0). Percentile ΔE is a probability function and can be interpreted as the percentage of the ΔE equal to or less than a specified amount. In Figure 2.18, 95% of ΔE_{00} measurements are equal to or less than 4.6 ΔE_{00}. Section 9.12 describes how percentile ΔE is used as a tolerance metric.

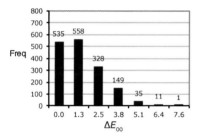
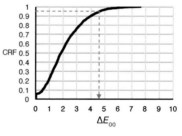

Figure 2.18.
Histogram and CRF of ΔE_{00}.

Mean is a measure of the color difference, with one-half of the color differences less than the average and the other half greater than the average. Yet visual color differences are associated with detecting large ΔE quantities. Therefore, using a larger percentage of the ΔE distribution, for example, the 95th percentile ΔE between two color characterization targets, to describe the color difference is more appropriate than using the mean ΔE (Chung and Shimamura, 2001).

2.22. Interpretation of ΔL^{*}, Δa^{*}, and Δb^{*}

ΔE, the color difference between a sample measurement and a target value, is a useful metric for conformity assessment. ΔE may not be useful for process control if the sources of variation are unknown. But the ΔE components—ΔL^{*}, Δa^{*}, and Δb^{*}—are indicative of what happens in the four-color printing process.

Table 2.4 is an interpretation of ΔL^{*}, Δa^{*}, and Δb^{*} between a sample and a reference (sample – reference). For example, when L^{*} of the sample minus the L^{*} of the reference is positive, the sample is lighter than the reference; when a^{*} of the sample minus the a^{*} of the reference is positive, the sample is redder or less green than the reference; and when b^{*} of the sample minus the b^{*} of the reference is positive, the sample is yellower or less blue than the reference. If we know the CIELAB values of the sample, we have the hue angle of the color, and that will further determine whether a color is redder or less green, and so on.

Table 2.4. Interpreting ΔL^*, Δa^*, and Δb^* between a sample and a reference (sample – reference).

When	The sample is
ΔL^* is positive	Lighter
ΔL^* is negative	Darker
Δa^* is positive	Redder or less green
Δa^* is negative	Less red and greener
Δb^* is positive	Yellower or less blue
Δb^* is negative	Less yellow or bluer

2.23. Viewing and Describing Color

Our visual system sees the color of interest in the context of its surroundings. A color-measuring instrument, however, measures color through an aperture. Thus, it excludes the influence of the surround. The two yellow patches shown in Figure 2.19 measure equally but appear to be different. The left patch with a green surround appears warmer and darker than the right patch with a blue surround. The phenomenon of "making one color looks like two" is called simultaneous contrast. In other words, "perception is reality" literally means that two colors, measured the same, are seen differently.

Figure 2.19.
An example of a simultaneous contrast.

Our visual system is very sensitive to small color differences when the colors of interest are viewed simultaneously. As shown in Figure 2.20, the color difference between Pantone 3955 and Pantone 3965 is hardly noticeable in the Adobe Color Picker when they are displayed next to each other with a gap (circled at left) but more noticeable when the two colors are juxtaposed (circled at right) without a gap.

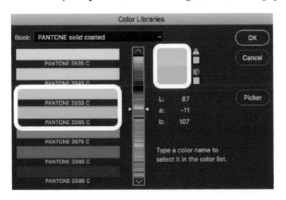

Figure 2.20.
Pantone 3955 and Pantone 3965 in Color Picker.

Printing-Process Control and Standardization

2.24. Color Constancy

If we photograph an object under three different lighting conditions and view the three pictures simultaneously, we may be surprised how different the color of the same object is. As shown in Figure 2.21, the letter-size board in the outdoor lighting with shade appears bluish gray; the same board in the tungsten lighting appears reddish gray; and the board in the standard graphic arts viewing booth appears neutral.

Figure 2.21.
Photographing an object in different light sources.

If we examine an object under a single light source, our visual system tends to discount the color and the intensity of the light. The discounting of the color or intensity of the light source in our visual system is called chromatic adaptation or lightness adaptation. The visual effect, or the tendency for objects to retain their color despite changes in illumination, is called color constancy (Hunt, 1987). The color constancy demonstration can be explained using the photograph of four women below.

Figure 2.22 (left) is a photograph of four women dressed in black, cyan, magenta, and yellow. If we want to change the color of the dress of the second woman from the left from cyan to green, we need to use the Selection Tool in Photoshop to isolate the color of the cyan dress in the image (Figure 2.22 right).

Overprinting yellow ink in the selection changes the dress from cyan to green (Figure 2.23 left). However, if we print the entire image with yellow ink, the dress remains as cyan, not green (Figure 2.23 right). Printing the entire image with the yellow ink is analogous to viewing or photographing the entire image in a yellowish lighting. The visual system adapts to the yellowish white point and never questions that the wall is not white. As a result, the dress remains as cyan. Chromatic adaptation happens very fast when the eye scans back and forth between the two images in Figure 2.23.

Figure 2.22.
An example of the chromatic adaptation. (Image courtesy of Erwin Widmer.)

Figure 2.23.
Applying yellow ink to the selection (left) and the entire image (right).

Figure 2.24 verifies that the green dress (left) and the cyan dress (right) are actually the same color when the surround is masked out with black paper. The black mask is intentionally made smaller than the image to indicate that Figure 2.24 and Figure 2.23 are the same images.

Figure 2.24.
The surround masked out with black paper.

Viewing the two small squares without the influence of the surround is similar to taking color measurement through a hold-down aperture. This is the fundamental difference between color perception (including surround influence) and color measurement (excluding surround influence).

2.25. Color Tolerance

Color matching is a special case of color difference, that is, the color difference is very small. But how small is small? Table 2.5 interprets ΔE according to the perceptibility and acceptability points of view. Perceptibility relates to the question "Can I tell the difference?" Acceptability answers the question "Can I accept the outcome?"

Table 2.5. Interpreting ΔE according to perceptibility and acceptability.

ΔE	Perceptibility	Acceptability
<1	No difference	Excellent match
1–2	Just noticeable	Good match
4–6	Noticeable	Fair match
>9	Strong difference	Poor match

When setting tolerances, the permissive color differences should be based on acceptability, not perceptibility. In addition, one should realize that the metrics specified will influence the assessment outcome. Specifically, the metrics, ΔL^*, Δa^*, and Δb^* define the shape of a cube; the metrics, ΔL^*, ΔC^*, and Δh, specify the shape of a wedge; and ΔE defines the shape of a sphere.

2.26. Communicating Color

Given the fact that the visual system is very sensitive when viewing two or more objects simultaneously, the following measures have been taken when communicating color in the printing industry:

1. Use Ishihara's color blindness test and the Farnsworth and Munsell 100-hue test to screen normal color vision.

2. Be aware that aging contributes to observer variation, particularly in differentiation of blues.

3. Use an ISO 3664-compliant light source to judge proof and print match (ISO, 2009c).

4. Use ISO 13655-compliant color-measurement devices to assess proofing and printing conformity (ISO, 2009b).

5. Use invariant match over metameric match for brand color match.

2.27. Device Color Space and Reference Color Space

Color is device dependent. This explains why different brands of color TV sets display the same broadcast signals differently. This also explains why the same broadcast signals, as displayed and as printed in magazines and newspapers, are different. For brand owners, significant color variations among different media are undesirable. They demand consistent color appearance across different media.

The solution to achieve consistent color appearance is to build look-up tables or profiles between device color spaces and a reference color space. For example, monitors can be calibrated to the sRGB color space (created by HP and Microsoft and widely used on the Internet), offset presses can be calibrated to a CMYK color space, and CIEXYZ and CIELAB can serve as the profile connection space. Similar to the airline industry, which uses a hub to serve many surrounding cities, source color can be translated into its destination via CIEXYZ and CIELAB color spaces. This will be discussed in chapter 3, "The ICC Color-Management System."

2.28. Chapter Summary

Color is a visual sensation resulting from the interaction of light, an object, and a human observer. Color can be measured numerically, and CIELAB is the device-independent color space, because it is based on imaginary primaries.

Colorimetry has multiple uses in graphic arts imaging practices. CIELAB color space is the language for color specifications. Color match can be invariant or metameric. Metamerism is both a blessing and a curse, because the match depends on either the light source or the observer.

The "Δ" is the quantitative difference between a sample and a reference. ΔC^*, a useful metric in ink formulation, is the difference in colorfulness between a sample and its reference. ΔC_h, a metric in gray balance assessment, is the difference in chroma between a near-neutral sample and its reference. Hue difference, ΔH^*, is the least-used metric. ΔE^*_{ab}, a metric in color matching, is the total color difference between a sample and a reference. ΔE_{00}, a more useful metric in color matching, is the total color difference between a sample and a reference, which correlates closely to visual perception. Color tolerance is influenced by the metrics as well as by its magnitude.

2.29. Multiple-Choice and Essay Questions

1. The 2° observer represents the _____ vision, which is a small area on the _____ with highest amount of red-, green-, and blue-sensitive cones.
   A. rod, retina
   B. fovea, retina
   C. retina, rod
   D. color, cornea

2. A spectral reflectance curve is unique to _____. The tristimulus values obtained from such data are _____ on the illuminant used.
   A. an object, independent
   B. a light source, dependent
   C. an object, dependent
   D. a light source, independent

3. CIE tristimulus values are the results of _____ three separate functions, and then _____ these quantities over the visible spectrum.
   A. adding, differentiating
   B. subtracting, integrating
   C. multiplying, integrating
   D. dividing, differentiating

4. The _____ of a color can be expressed as the wavelength of the spectrum color whose chromaticity coordinates are on the same straight line as the sample and the illuminant point.
   A. hue
   B. saturation
   C. purity
   D. lightness

5. What can be said about two colors that have the same coordinates in the CIE a^*b^* diagram, but with different L^* values?
   A. They have the same hue angle
   B. ΔE is 0 between them
   C. They are metamers
   D. They match invariantly

6. _____, adopted in 1976, is a uniform color space that uses opponent color coordinates to arrange colors according to their psychophysical parameters.
   A. The chromaticity diagram
   B. The Munsell color system
   C. The CIELAB color system
   D. The RIT process ink gamut chart

7. Given that the ΔE between C_1 and C_2 is 10 and the ΔE between C_1 and C_3 is 5, what is the ΔE between C_2 and C_3?

A. 5

B. 15

C. square root of the sum of 10^2 and 5^2

D. unknown

8. Two objects with identical spectrophotometric curves _____.

A. have the same color

B. are metamers

C. may not match in color

D. have different ΔE values under different illuminants

9. The color science community became aware of the issue of uniform color space through _____.

A. tristimulus integration

B. metamerism

C. MacAdam ellipses

D. RGB-to-CMYK color conversion

10. The CIELAB value of the color known as "fire-engine red" will have _____.

A. a^* and b^* near zero

B. a large value for C^*

C. a hue angle near 180°

D. negative a^* and b^* values

11. Why is metamerism a blessing *and* a curse?

12. Point out the difference between the two parameters, ΔC^* and ΔC_h^*.

3   The ICC Color-Management System

The color-management system (CMS) is about managing the print media process and involves more than separating color into CMYK channels, putting dots on plates, and transferring ink to paper. The International Color Consortium (ICC) believes that color management must be addressed at the operating system (OS) level, and not at the applications level. After reading this chapter, one should know how we managed color before the days of ICC, and the key components and actions in the ICC color management.

3.1.   Color Management before the Days of ICC

Before the ICC was founded, a graphic arts system might be characterized by film-based color separation using a camera/enlarger and manual page assembly and platemaking, plus sheetfed offset printing. Later, film-based color separation was replaced by electronic dot generation scanners in the 1980s. Manual page assembly and platemaking were replaced by CEPS (color electronic prepress systems) and CTP (computer-to-plate) devices in the 1990s. The print media market remained the dominant form of mass communication (no Internet then), and high-speed web offset presses further pushed the graphic arts system toward shorter cycle times and greater productivity. While capital investments, for example, buying bigger and faster printing equipment, often helped solve productivity issues, they did not solve quality issues.

Figure 3.1 is a generic color-imaging system, which consisted of many diverse components. Input devices (e.g., scanners and digital cameras) captured digital images in RGB color space. But RGB was not clearly defined, and as a result, digital data exchange between different brands of equipment became a nightmare.

In the early days, display devices were monochrome, which was sufficient for typesetting and text composition purposes. Color images were handled separately and combined with the texts by double-burns during film-based platemaking. Later, color displays became the "output" of a CEPS but had no connection to the actual printing conditions. Thus, what one saw on the monitor was not the same as what would be printed.

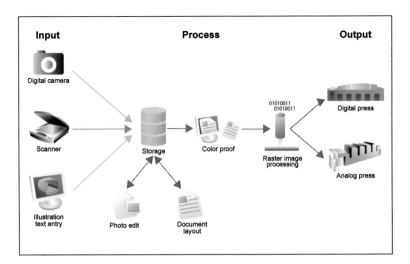

Figure 3.1.
A generic color-imaging system.

It was understood that different hard-copy output devices would reproduce the same CMYK separation differently. It was the responsibility of the prepress house or the printer to reconcile the color differences by using their craftsmanship to match customer-supplied proofs during printing. In other words, poor device-to-device color agreement existed before the introduction of ICC color management. Craftsmanship was often used to fix color-related problems, but could not prevent these problems. This chapter focuses on color-management solutions, that is, achieving color agreement systematically, by eliminating color-related mistakes, waste, and frustration.

3.2. Device-Dependent Color-Management Solutions

During the development of CEPS in the 1990s, color management was envisioned as a solution between a fixed input (RGB) device and a fixed output (CMYK) device. This pair-wise color-management solution, like a highway system confined to an island, was effective only within its boundaries, and the digital assets could not be repurposed outside the system's constraints. In addition, the number of possible pairs from any input to any output is large. As shown in Figure 3.2, there are (3 × 4) or 12 conversions between three input devices and four output devices.

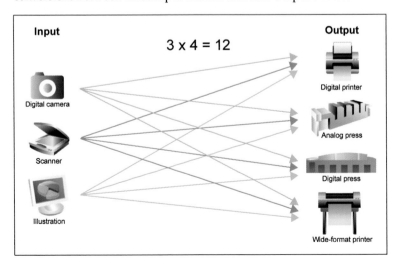

Figure 3.2.
Device-dependent color-management model.

3.3. Device-Independent Color-Management Solutions

The purpose of ICC was to create and promote the standardization of an open, vendor-neutral CMS by making color seamless between devices and documents. The ICC website (www.color.org), Figure 3.3, contains a wealth of up-to-date information, including ICC specifications, technical notes, white papers, registered profiles, and user forums, for system developers and end users.

Figure 3.3.
International Color
Consortium (ICC)
website logo.

An idea behind ICC color management is to decouple input–output pairs by connecting every device to a device-independent color space (Figure 3.4). A hub, namely the CIELAB color space, serves as a bridge between imaging devices. The connection between the device color space and the CIELAB color space is called a profile. In this approach, the number of conversions is reduced from (3 × 4) to (3 + 4), or 7.

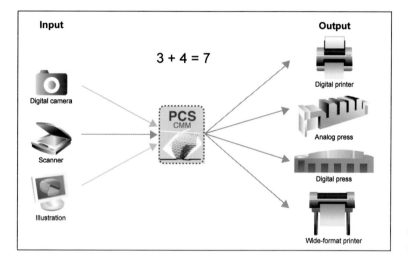

Figure 3.4.
Device-independent
color-management
model.

3.4. CMS Components

Figure 3.5 is a CMS model consisting of an application programming interface (API), images to be converted (left), ICC profile of the source color space, profile connection space (PCS), color-management module (CMM), ICC profile of the destination color space, and converted images (right). These diverse components work together and make for seamless color conversion between different OSs, software applications, and imaging devices.

Figure 3.5.
CMS components.

3.5. Profile, PCS, CMM, and API

An ICC profile defines the relationship between device values (RGB or CMYK) and actual colors that these devices produce. In other words, a profile consists of look-up tables (LUTs) that are unique to the device. The device space is known as the "A" space. The PCS, the "B" space, is the conduit for color conversion. Figure 3.5 shows the A-to-B conversion from RGB space to CIELAB space, and the B-to-A conversion from CIELAB space to CMYK space. Together, the color conversion is also known as the A-to-B-to-A conversion.

An ICC profile of a CMYK printer describes the relationship between its CMYK values and the CIELAB values. The ICC profile of a CMYK printer is device dependent, including not only hardware, but also consumables. Thus, the printer ICC profile works best at its calibrated state.

The CMM, a software engine, uses two profiles—a source profile and a destination profile—to convert color images pixel by pixel. The source profile is used to perform the A-to-B conversion; and the destination profile is used to perform the B-to-A conversion according to a specified color-rendering intent.

The API, application programming interface, provides color rendering to application software using a standard architecture and profile format.

Principles, tools, and practices of ICC color management are covered in greater details in publications by Fraser (2005), Sharma (2018), etc.

3.6. Printer-profiling Targets

Printer profiling requires significant resources, that is, a printer-profiling target, a pressrun, a color-measurement instrument, and profiling software. There was no standard profiling target in the 1990s. Color-management software vendors had to create their own printer-profiling targets. This meant a demand for valuable printing resources and associated color-measurement tasks in user communities. This was a challenge until the printer-profiling target was standardized by the American National Standards Institute Committee for Graphic Arts Technology Standards (ANSI/CGATS) (the target is called IT8.7/4) and, later, by ISO with 1617 patches. Figure 3.6 is the ISO 12642-2 printer-profiling target in a visual layout (ISO, 2005b).

3.7. Color Rendering Intents

There are different color rendering intents between device values and colorimetric values to address the gamut compression issue in the B-to-A conversion. Three rendering intents or LUTs are required in an ICC profile: 0 for perceptual rendering, 1 for colorimetric rendering, and 2 for saturation rendering.

Perceptual rendering, denoted as "B2A0," preserves the overall color appearance and the color relationships while the gamut is compressed between the source and the destination. Perceptual rendering is suitable for rendering pictorial color images that contain many out-of-gamut colors, one example being the conversion from the sRGB color space to a CMYK color space.

Relative colorimetric rendering, denoted as "B2A1," ignores the white point of the source profile, but recognizes the white point of the destination profile. For example, in the sRGB-to-CMYK conversion, the relative colorimetric rendering ignores the white point of the sRGB ($100L^*$,

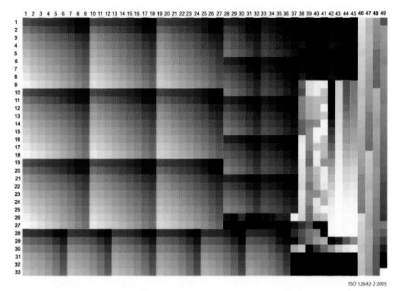

Figure 3.6.
ISO 12642-2
printer-profiling
target in visual layout.
(Reproduced with
permission from
ANSI on behalf of ISO.

$0a^*$, $0b^*$) and maps the white point to the device values of the CMYK substrate (C0, M0, Y0, K0). In addition, relative colorimetric rendering also matches the reproducible colors and clips out-of-gamut colors.

Absolute colorimetric rendering recognizes the white point of the source and maps the white point of the source to its destination. For example, in the color proofing workflow or CMYK-to-CMYK conversion, absolute colorimetric rendering recognizes the white point of the source CMYK (this is paper color of the printer space) and matches it to the destination CMYK (this is the proofer space). Absolute colorimetric rendering also matches reproducible colors and clips out-of-gamut colors.

Saturation rendering, denoted as "B2A2," assumes that the destination color space is larger than the source. It addresses gamut expansion instead of gamut clipping, expanding colors in the source to the destination to produce more vivid colors. Saturation rendering is suitable for pie charts and other business graphics applications.

3.8. Device Gamut and Rendering

The difference between device gamuts is like the difference between a house and an apartment. Perceptual rendering intent, particularly the B-to-A conversion, may be compared to moving furniture (tables and chairs) from a house to an apartment. The starting point is the furniture in a large house, where there is plenty of space between items. When moving to a space-limited apartment, there are different approaches to handling the furniture. First, we can get rid of some furniture and move only the essential pieces to the apartment. This is analogous to perceptual rendering. Second, we can move all the furniture to the apartment, but soon we realize that we have run out of space and need to pile extra furniture up in the hallway. This is analogous to the colorimetric rendering, in which out-of-gamut colors are clipped.

When gamut clipping is inevitable, there are different gamut mapping approaches to (1) preserve the hue, (2) preserve the lightness, and (3) achieve the least ΔE. There is no easy way to find out how gamut clipping is handled by software, and extensive testing is necessary.

3.9. Color-Management Actions

Adobe Photoshop and other Adobe Creative Suite software are good examples of ICC color-management applications. There are four major color-management actions: (1) selecting color settings, (2) assigning a profile, (3) embedding a profile, and (4) converting with a profile. Examples from Photoshop are used to explain how these color-management actions work.

3.10. Color Settings

As shown in Figure 3.7, Photoshop, Edit > Color Settings, offers regional (European, North American, Japanese) color settings. Specifically, the European Prepress 3 CMYK working space is set to coated FOGRA39, the North America Prepress 2 CMYK working space is set to U.S. web coated (SWOP), and Japan's Prepress 2 CMYK working space is set to Japan Color 2001 coated. Regional color settings can be altered by the user and saved as Custom color settings (e.g., My Color Settings).

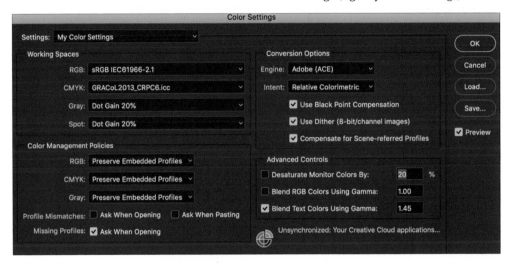

Figure 3.7.
Color settings in Adobe Photoshop.

Using Figure 3.7 to elaborate, if a new RGB file is created, it will have the sRGB.icc profile assigned to it. If this is a CMYK file type, it will have the GRACoL2013_CRPC6.icc profile assigned to the image.

Color-management policies offer the option to (1) preserve, (2) convert to working space, or (3) turn the profile off. "Preserve" means to preserve the embedded profile in a newly opened document if the profile does not match the working space. "Convert to working space" means to preserve the color appearance by converting the document to the working space. "Off" means ignoring the embedded profile if it differs from the working space, and the numeric values of the file remain the same.

Conversion options offer CMM and rendering intent choices. Adobe calls CMM Color Engine and recommends its own Adobe Color Engine. In a pictorial color image reproduction workflow, the relative colorimetric rendering intent and the black point compensation are recommended. The effect is that the source (sRGB) white point of (R255, G255, B255) is mapped to the destination (CMYK) white point (C0, M0, Y0, K0).

3.11. Assigning a Profile

Assigning a profile provides color definition to the device values in the image (Figure 3.8). If "Don't color manage this document" is chosen, Photoshop uses the working space as the default ICC profile for the image.

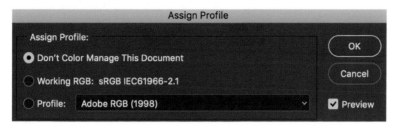

Figure 3.8.
Assign Profile in Adobe Photoshop.

Using the color settings in Figure 3.7 and RGB values of (R200, G100, B50) as an example, if you select "assigning the working space (sRGB)," Photoshop will display the color the same as "Don't color manage this document." But if other RGB color spaces, for example, ColorMatch RGB, Apple RGB, or Adobe RGB (1998), are assigned to the image, Assign Profile will change the color appearance of the file, but not the numeric values of the file (Figure 3.9).

sRGB   ColorMatch RGB   Apple RGB   Adobe RGB

Figure 3.9.
Effect of assigning different RGB working spaces.

Using the color settings in Figure 3.7 and a CMYK pictorial color image as an example, assigning different CMYK working spaces to a file will change the color appearance of the image, but not the numeric CMYK values in the file. As shown in Figure 3.10, the image on the left simulates the CRPC2 (a smaller color gamut) printing, and the image on the right simulates the CRPC6 (a larger color gamut) printing. This means that the colors of the vegetables are duller when reproduced in the CRPC2 printing conditions and more vivid in the CRPC6 printing conditions.

CRPC2   CRPC6

Figure 3.10.
Effect of assigning two different CMYK working spaces.

3.12. Embedding a Profile

Adobe Photoshop handles embedding or not embedding a profile for the image when saving the file. Embedding a profile for the image provides color portability by informing the receiver of the document what the color space of the document is. Embedding a profile is suitable for raw color images or images that were already color managed and are to be further processed in the workflow. Embedding a profile is not suitable for test targets (e.g., color control bar, color characterization target), because they represent device values only.

3.13. Converting with a Profile

Two profiles, a source profile and a destination profile, are required when converting a color document. The source profile represents the color space of the input device, defined by the A-to-B tag. The destination profile, defined by the B-to-A tag, represents the color space of the output device according to a rendering intent. Figure 3.11 is an example of color conversion from an sRGB color space to a CMYK-GRACoL2013_CRPC6 color space. It is denoted as "A2B2A." In this case, the color conversion changes RGB numbers to CMYK numbers in the digital file according to the GRACoL_CRPC6 definition using Relative Colorimetric rendering intent plus the Black Point Compensation.

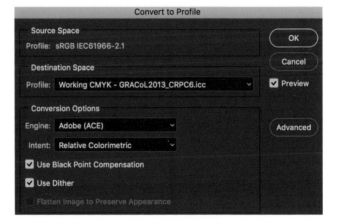

Figure 3.11. Converting with profiles in Adobe Photoshop.

In the publication printing industry, the B-to-A conversion processes job data from the PCS to CMYK color space to be printed by web offset presses. In the transactional printing market, the B-to-A conversion processes job data from the PCS to CMYK space to be printed by digital presses.

3.14. Device-Link Profile

Two ICC profiles are used to transform between device value and PCS. A device-link profile transforms directly from one set of CMYK data to another set of CMYK data. Device-link profiles are used to implement a digital proofing workflow. Figure 3.12 shows (1) how color-managed CMYK images are printed in standard printing conditions, and (2) how a device-link profile is used to convert the standard CMYK data to the proofer data so that the proof matches the standard print.

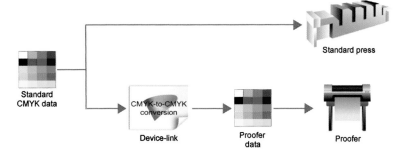

Figure 3.12.
Device-link profile
in a digital proofing
workflow.

For in-gamut colors, the same color can be produced with various combinations of CMYK tone values. Because black ink costs less than chromatic (CMY) inks, device-link profiles are also used for ink optimization (high GCR) and high-volume color printing scenarios.

3.15.   Color-Management Challenges

Color-management challenges are about managing changes in the color reproduction workflow. The success of color management depends on rigor of planning, device calibration, device profiling, color conversion, and printing-process control, denoted by the inner circle of Figure 3.13.

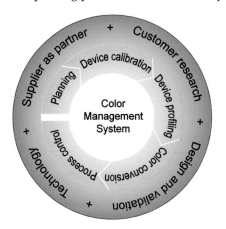

Figure 3.13.
Color management
and the extended
print media.

Device calibration adjusts color input devices and output devices to conform to specifications, and is verified periodically. Device profiling is not required for printing presses that have been calibrated to standards (ISO 12647-2 [ISO, 2013a], GRACoL 2013, etc.), because standard ICC profiles are available free of charge from the ICC Profile Registrar. However, device profiling is necessary for digital color proofers, particularly device-link profiles, to produce color proofs that match the press sheets. Printing-process control requires the use of color measurement as a feedback loop to ensure the repeatability of the printing process as calibrated.

Color-management challenges are about managing the extended process, and involve understanding customer's needs and wants, design and validation, technological advancements, and supplier as partner, as denoted by the outer circle of Figure 3.13. Color management needs to take into consideration device binding (when to convert in the workflow), digital asset storage/retrieval (cloud computing), and repurposing for other media uses.

Color-management challenges are about managing the expectations of print buyers and designers. When reproducing pictorial images from an RGB color space to a CMYK color space, it should be clearly communicated that, for the most part, the goal is an attractive print product, not an exact match of the source RGB images. One may ask, "When does 'color image match' become an important matter?" The answer is "Between color proofs and press sheets." This is where we build the device-link between the standard CMYK (source) and the proofer (destination) in the color proofing workflow.

Looking ahead, paper stock preference, including paper containing an optical brightening agent (OBA), represents another change in customer expectation that we need to address. This topic will be covered in chapter 9, "Printing Standards in a Changing Industry."

3.16. Chapter Summary

There are four major color-management actions: (1) selecting color settings, (2) assigning a profile, (3) embedding a profile, and (4) converting with a profile. Color settings denote preferences in working spaces and color-management policies. Assigning a profile to an image starts the color-management journey. Converting an image from one device color space to the other is workflow dependent. Achieving good color image reproduction is the goal of converting from an RGB to a CMYK color space. Achieving a color image match is the goal of color proofing. Embedding a profile for an image enables it to make its color-management journey independent of file location.

3.17. Multiple-Choice and Essay Questions

1. _____ involves establishing a fixed, repeatable condition for an input or an output device, and any variables that might alter the color of the image must be identified and secured.
A. Calibration
B. Characterization
C. Profiling
D. Color conversion

2. Which one is least like the other three?
A. sRGB
B. ColorMatch RGB
C. SWOP
D. Adobe RGB

3. Which rendering style accounts for the white point of the source?
A. Perceptual
B. Relative colorimetric
C. Absolute colorimetric
D. Saturation

4. The ICC color management system helps simplify color conversion tasks from ($n \times m$) number of conversions to _____ number of conversions.
A. ($m + n$)
B. (m/n)
C. ($m + n$)/2
D. ($m - n$)

5. _____ is not required for printing presses that have been calibrated to standards, because standard ICC profiles are available from the ICC Profile Registrar.
A. Device calibration
B. Device profiling
C. Color proofing
D. Raster image processing

6. _____ acts as the color transformation engine in an ICC CMS.
A. CMM
B. API
C. Scanner profile
D. Data file

7. The profile connection space (PCS) _____.
A. refers to the junction where different device profiles are cross-referenced
B. describes the standard monitor viewing conditions
C. requires at least three profiles to make the conversion
D. All of the above

8. In order to _____ digital proofers, these devices must first be _____ to a known state of operation.
A. calibrate, characterized
B. characterize, calibrated
C. reduce dot gain of, characterized
D. maximize ink trapping, profiled

9. Which ICC rendering style is most suitable for color rendering of RGB-to-CMYK images for publication printing?
A. Perceptual
B. Relative densitometric
C. Absolute colorimetric
D. Saturation

10. _____ causes the same CMYK image to appear differently in different CMYK working spaces.
A. Embedding a profile
B. Assigning a profile
C. Converting a profile
D. All of the above

11. Why is a CMYK printer profile device dependent?

12. What happens to a RGB image file and its display in Adobe Photoshop when the Assign Profile command is used?

4 Printing Standardization

Standard development is based on the consensus of different parties, including users, interest groups, and standards organizations. This chapter covers standardization and its benefits, graphic technology standard organizations at different organizational levels, how standards are developed, and some applicable printing standards.

4.1. Standardization and Its Benefits

One may argue that standardization suppresses creativity and stifles innovation. But it is the premise of this book that standardization helps maximize compatibility, interoperability, safety, and quality. By addressing common needs and specifying key requirements, standardization facilitates the manufacturing of goods by defining product specifications that are accepted in the markets.

Standards touch lives at work and play. Today, modern citizens benefit from using wireless mobile communication devices for shopping, dining, transportation, and entertainment expenses. Travelers benefit from using credit cards and not being concerned with currency exchanges at borders.

Without standardization, a company's product line must span an entire system, because individual components from different competitors would be incompatible. But with standardization, a company can focus on providing an individual component of a system and allowing products to be produced in the most cost-effective manners, making them more attractive to consumers and promoting economic growth.

Print buyers need to manage complex supply chains around the globe. They benefit from standardization because product quality can be assessed and verified in different locations and at different times. Standards also contribute to the sustainability of growth by insuring that products will be safe to use, and that the processes used to make them will protect the environment.

4.2. Printing Industry Stakeholders

The business of printing, like any other business, is made up of the supply side and the demand side. The demand side (or the print buyer) has needs and wants. The supply side (or the printer) has resources and expertise to satisfy these needs and wants. Together, they are the stakeholders who share a vital interest in the business and its activities.

Figure 4.1 illustrates many stakeholders and their interactions in the printing industry. Print buyers and designers represent the demand side of the industry. Prepress operators, plate makers, printers, and postpress operators represent the supply side of the industry. The stakeholders in the printing industry may be extended to include suppliers, industry associations, local and federal governments.

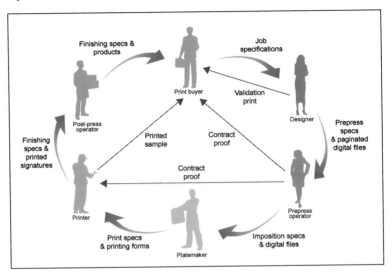

Figure 4.1.
Printing industry stakeholders.

When interpreting stakeholders in the newspaper industry, the print buyer includes the newspaper publisher and businesses who purchase advertising spaces. The printer, typically, is a part of the newspaper organization. The *New York Times,* the *Boston Globe,* and the *Washington Post* are examples of newspaper publishers in the United States. Materials and processes used in publishing newspapers are well defined in terms of page size, color, finishing, and delivery. To meet the high-volume needs, short cycle time, and drive print manufacturing costs down, newspaper printing standards have been developed for web offset printing presses.

When interpreting stakeholders in the magazine publication industry, the print buyer is the publisher and businesses who purchase advertising pages. The printer is usually a separate business entity who is contracted for two to three years at a time to do the print fulfillment. Time, Inc. is an example of a magazine publisher who publishes *Time* magazine and *Fortune* magazine weekly. R.R. Donnelly and Quad Graphics are examples of printers who specialize in magazine and catalog printing. To meet high-volume needs, the materials, proofing, and printing processes (e.g., Grade 3 and Grade 5 papers, web offset presses) are also standardized in terms of size, color, bindery, and finishing.

When interpreting stakeholders in the commercial printing industry, there are many print buyers, and their needs vary. For example, business cards are an example of a commercial printing job with a short lead time and a short print run. Another example is a new car brochure, which incorporates the creative procedures of an advertising agency. Commercial printers have to use a variety of inks, substrates, presses, and operators' know-how to meet their customers' needs. By collaborating with major stakeholders, commercial printing standards have been developed, based on the standard process inks, Grade 1 papers, and sheetfed offset presses.

When interpreting stakeholders in the label and packaging printing industry, the print buyer is, typically, a brand owner who often hires a design agency to create new packages, labels, or sales brochures. The design process is often iterated until a validation print or a comprehensive (also known as a comp) is accepted by the print buyer. Based on the comp and the digital file, the prepress operator produces a contract proof and sends it to the brand owner for approval. Once the contract proof is approved, the platemaker receives the digital file and uses imposition software and CTP (computer-to-plate) equipment to make printing plates specifically for the configuration of a printing press. The printer receives the contract proof, the plates, and the printing specifications. If the brand color is specified with a tight tolerance, the printer should reproduce the brand color using a separate printing unit and a specially formulated ink. The printed sample is sent to the brand owner to close the job (and get paid), while the postpress operator turns printed signatures into finished products for distribution.

4.3. Technology Standard Organizations

There are three levels of standardization activities around the world: (1) industry level, where regional standards are developed; (2) national level, where national standards are developed; and (3) international level, where one standard and one test method are accepted everywhere. An example of each of the technology standards organizations is discussed in the following sections.

4.4. Industry-Level Organization: Idealliance

Idealliance, based in Alexandria, VA, is an industry association representing the visual communications industry in the United States. The stakeholders include content and media creators, print and digital service providers, material suppliers, and technology partners. Idealliance publishes print media methodologies, specifications, and standards, including SWOP®, GRACoL®, and G7® (Idealliance, 2014).

SWOP® stands for Specifications for Web Offset Publications. SWOP was a color reproduction specification for web offset lithography in 1975. It became CGATS TR 001 (CGATS, 1995). Today, there are two SWOP specifications. SWOP3 specification is for printing on Grade 3 paper, and SWOP5 specification is for printing on Grade 5 paper. SWOP printing aims, a color characterization data set, are specified by CGATS TR 003 and CGATS TR 005 reference printing conditions, respectively.

GRACoL® stands for the General Requirements for Applications in Commercial Offset Lithography. GRACoL is a color reproduction specification for sheetfed offset lithography using ISO 2846-1 (ISO, 2006) conformed process inks and ISO 12647-2 conformed Grade 1 or Grade 2 papers (ISO, 2013a). GRACoL printing aims, a color characterization data set, are specified by CGATS TR 006 reference printing conditions. Idealliance no longer specifies solid ink density and TVI as printing aims. But printers and consultants often use densitometric tools and metrics in routine production work.

G7® is both a specification of grayscale appearance and a press calibration method for adjusting any CMYK imaging device to conform to the G7 grayscale metrics (Idealliance, 2018). G7 yields a visual match between different imaging systems, including substrate colors, using 1-D transfer curves without ICC color management.

Other industry-level standards organizations include Fogra and bvdm in Germany (bvdm, 2016), Ugra in Switzerland, BPiF in the United Kingdom, etc. While much 4-color work is exported from Asia, there is no printing-specific organization in Asia, but printing experts working under the auspices of their national standards organizations.

4.5. National-Level Organization: U.S. CGATS

CGATS, Committee for Graphic Arts Technology Standards, was formed in 1987 by the American National Standards Institute (ANSI; www.ansi. org). The goal of CGATS is to have all technical work for printing, publishing, and conversion technologies represented in one national standardization and coordination effort.

Headquartered in Reston, VA, CGATS provides a vehicle for other industry organizations (e.g., Idealliance) to work under the CGATS "umbrella," enabling them to move their industry standards into the national standards arena and have the work developed and approved as ANSI CGATS standards.

CGATS is made up of the ASC (Accredited Standards Committee) and TAG (Technical Advisory Group). CGATS has developed standards relating to metrology, terminology, process control, color data definition, and digital data exchange. All standards undergo a periodic review every 5 years to determine whether to reaffirm, revise, or withdraw the standard. CGATS also acts as a liaison for international standards development.

4.6. International-Level Organization: ISO

The International Organization for Standardization (ISO) organizes its technical work through its technical management board (TMB). The TMB is responsible for the establishment of technical committees (TC); appointment of chairpersons and secretariats of technical committees, and approval of titles and scopes of work of technical committees (ISO, 2011a).

Located in Geneva, Switzerland, ISO develops consensus-driven, widely recognized standards. Consensus, which requires the resolution of substantial objections, is a necessary condition for the approval of international standards.

ISO/TC 130 addresses standardization in the field of printing and graphic technologies (McDowell, 1996). This field covers all phases of the process in which graphic elements are created, manipulated, assembled, communicated, and finally delivered electronically as digital products or physically to substrates using inks, toners, and finishes as demanded by the end applications.

ISO/TC 130 standards include, but are not limited to, those of terminology; evaluation of visual appearance of product quality; data exchange; process control; conformity assessment; impacts on the environment; and requirements for and testing of related materials, equipment, and systems.

4.7. ISO/TC 130: Graphic Technology

ISO/TC 130 milestone events in the past 40 years include, but are not limited to, the following: (1) TC130, created in 1969, but soon became dormant; (2) CEPS (color electronic prepress system), introduced in 1979, but lacking data exchange standards; (3) DDES (digital data exchange standards) work started in 1982 by exchanging device values via magnetic tapes; (4) color characterization targets (IT8.7/1, IT8.7/2, and IT8.7/3) introduced in 1988; and (5) reactivated in Berlin, Germany, in 1989 (McDowell, 1999).

As of 2020, there are 21 countries registered as P-members and 24 countries registered as O-members. P-members require active participation in the committee activities, pay membership dues, and have voting rights. O-members are observers of the committee activities, do not pay membership dues, and do not have voting rights. A total of 101 ISO standards have been published by ISO/TC 130.

ISO/TC 130 develops its standards through the following working groups (WG), joint work groups (JWG) with other TCs, and task forces (TF):

WG1 Terminology
WG2 Prepress data exchange
WG3 Process control & related metrology
WG4 Media & materials
WG5 Ergonomics and safety
JWG7 Color management
JWG10 Management of security printing processes
WG11 Environmental impacts of graphic technology
WG12 Postpress
WG13 Printing conformity assessment requirements
JWG14 Print-quality measurement methods

4.8. Standards Development Process

According to the *ISO/IEC Directives, Part 1, Procedures for the Technical Work* (ISO, 2011a), there are a number of project stages in ISO standards development. Table 4.1 shows the sequence of project stages through which the technical work is developed, and gives the name of the document associated with each project stage.

Table 4.1. ISO project stages and associated documents.

Project stage	Associated documents	
	Name	**Abbreviation**
Preliminary	Preliminary work item	PWI
Proposal	New work item proposal	NP
Preparatory	Working draft	WD
Committee	Committee draft	CD
Enquiry	Draft international standard	DIS
Approval	Final draft international standard	FDIS
Publication	International standard	IS

To elaborate, a WG may introduce a preliminary work item (PWI). The PWI must be documented and fully justified before progressing to the next stage, that is, it must be approved by at least four P-members in the technical committee (TC). At the proposal stage, the NP must be approved by a simple majority of the P-members of the TC.

At the preparatory stage, the goal is to seek consensus and resolve differences from national bodies by revising and enhancing working drafts (WD). At the committee draft (CD) stage, the goal is to seek consensus and resolve differences among experts who serve on the committee. CD may take several iterations of deliberating and editing before reaching the next stage.

At the enquiry stage, a draft international standard (DIS) is circulated. A positive vote may be accompanied by editorial or technical comments. A negative vote must be accompanied by technical reasons. The DIS is approved if a two-thirds majority of the votes cast by the P-members of the technical committee are in favor.

At the approval stage, the final draft international standard (FDIS) must be distributed to national bodies for a vote. If a national body votes affirmatively, no technical comments are allowed. If a national body finds an FDIS unacceptable, it votes negatively and must state the technical reasons. The FDIS is optional if a two-thirds majority of the votes cast by the P-members of the technical committee in the DIS vote are in favor.

At the publication stage, ISO will finalize the document, indicated by the secretariat of the technical committee, and print and distribute the International Standard (IS) within 2 months.

4.9. ISO Verbs and Deliverables

ISO documents use the following verbs to differentiate a requirement from a recommendation. The word *shall* indicates a requirement or must comply. The word *should* indicates a recommendation or nice to comply. The word *may,* indicates a permission, and the word *can,* indicates a possibility.

ISO publishes four types of publications. An International Standard (IS) contains normative requirements and must be approved by a two-thirds majority of the P-members, and that not more than one-quarter of the total number of votes cast are negative. Other ISO deliverables, explained below, do not contain normative requirements, and the approval process is less stringent.

Technical Specifications (TS) represent an agreement among the members of a TC, but not an agreement to publish an IS. TS must be approved by two-thirds of the P-members. For example, ISO/TS 10128 *Graphic Technology—Methods of Adjustment of the Colour Reproduction of a Printing System to Match a Set of Characterization Data,* is a TS (ISO, 2015a). TS is used for "pre-standardization purposes" and an explanation of its relationship to the expected future IS should be mentioned in the foreword.

A Technical Report (TR) contains informative requirements, as opposed to normative requirements. A TR requires simple majority approval by the P-members. For example, ISO/TR 19300.4 *Graphic Technology—Guidelines for the Use of Standards for Print Media Production Workflows,* is a TR (ISO, 2015e).

A Public Available Specification (PAS) may be an intermediate specification, published before the development of a full IS. A PAS requires simple majority approval by the P-members. For example, ISO/PAS 15339-1 *Graphic Technology—Printing from Digital Data across Multiple Technologies—Part 1: Principles,* is a PAS (ISO, 2015c).

4.10. Applicable Printing Standards

A technical standard consists of an introduction, scope, terminology, and requirements. Requirements address test methods, sampling, metrology, aims, and tolerances. In this book, applicable printing standards are grouped into the following categories: (1) color definition, (2) color measurement, (3) visual inspection, and (4) color reproduction.

1. In the color definition category, digital files are prepared in accordance with ISO 15930-7 *Graphic Technology—PDF/X-4* (ISO, 2007b). Spot color definitions follow ISO 17972-4 *Graphic Yechnology—CXF/X-4 Spot Color Characterization Data* (ISO, 2011c). A validation print that is supplied by a print buyer to a print service provider should adhere to ISO 12647-8 *Graphic Technology—Validation Print Processes Working Directly from Digital Data* (ISO, 2012c). Soft proofing should be in agreement with ISO 12646 *Graphic Technology—Displays for Color Proofing* (ISO, 2006), and ISO 14861 *Graphic Technology—Requirements for Colour Soft Proofing Systems* (ISO, 2013b). A hard proof that is supplied by a print buyer to a print service provider should be in agreement with ISO 12647-7 *Graphic Technology—Proofing Processes Working Directly from Digital Data* (ISO, 2015b).

2. In the color-measurement category, ISO 13655 specifies 0°:45° or 45°:0° measurement geometry, 2° standard observer, D50 standard illuminant, CIELAB color system, and matte white backing for the specimen (ISO, 2009b). It also specifies M1 measurement mode with a known amount of UV component in measurement source. Annex 4 of ISO 13655 introduces a tristimulus linear-correction method to correct measurement backing difference. The method was extended to correct printing aims due to paper color difference, as discussed in section 9.7, "What's SCCA?"

3. In the visual inspection category, ISO 3664 specifies the D50 (5,000 K) illuminant with a high illuminance of 2,000 lux for critical color matching appraisal, as well as an illumination of 500 lux for practical color appraisal (ISO, 2009a). Section 9.13 also discusses the revision of ISO 3664 in more detail.

4. In the color reproduction category, we can further divide printing standards into three sections: (a) press calibration methods, (b) digital printing standards, and (c) analog printing standards. Press calibration methods will be discussed in chapter 6, "Device Calibration." Digital printing standards will be discussed in chapter 9, "Printing Standards in a Changing Industry." Analog printing standards will be discussed in the remainder of this chapter.

4.11. ISO 12647-2: Process Control for Offset Lithographic Processes

First published in 1996, ISO 12647-2 is one of the eight-part process control standards. ISO 12647-2 recognizes the substrate, process ink, halftone screening, and inking sequence as primary process control parameters. The standard was revised in 2004 to include solid coloration and TVI for five print substrates (PS) and printing conditions (PC).

ISO 12647-2 was revised again in 2013 to include eight paper specifications and printing conditions (ISO, 2013a). It removed film-based TVI requirements and defined TVI aims based on CTP linear plates. It included the M1 measurement condition and ΔE_{00} (informative) metric. Additionally, it recognized the gray reproduction metric (ΔC_h) in addition to MTS (ISO, 2013a).

ISO 12647-2 specifies the following aspects of process control for standardizing sheetfed and web offset printing:

1. Print substrate (PS): There are eight print substrates (PS1–PS8) specifications, including paper surface, mass per area, whiteness, gloss, color, and fluorescence. Table 4.2 illustrates PS1, also known as the premium coated or Grade 1, specifications. Notice that the paper has a negative b^* value due to the presence of optical brightening agents (OBA).

Table 4.2. ISO 12647-2 print substrate (PS1) specifications.

Type of surface	Premium coated
Mass per area	80–250 (115) g/m²
Whiteness	105–135
Gloss	10–80
Color	95L^*, 1a^*, −4b^* (white backing) 93L^*, 1a^*, −5b^* (black backing)
Tolerance	±3L^*/±2a^*/±4b^*
Fluorescence	moderate

2. Coloration description (CD): There are eight coloration descriptions (CD1–CD8), including solid colorations of CMYKRGB on each print substrate. Table 4.3 illustrates CD1 specifications, including white-backing (WB) and black-backing (BB) colorimetric aims. Because paper is translucent, color measurement is affected by measurement backing more for bright inks than dark-colored inks. In this case, the yellow solid has less L^* and less C^* in the black-backing measurement condition.

Table 4.3. ISO 12647-2 coloration description (CD1) specifications.

	White backing			Black backing		
Color	L^*	a^*	b^*	L^*	a^*	b^*
K	16	0	0	16	0	0
C	56	−36	−51	55	−35	−51
M	48	75	−4	47	73	−4
Y	89	−4	93	87	−4	91
R	48	68	47	46	67	45
G	50	−65	26	49	−63	25
B	25	20	−46	24	20	−45
CMY	23	0	−1	23	0	−1

3. Printing condition (PC): There are eight printing conditions (PC1–PC8), including two TVIs (periodic and nonperiodic screening) for each printing condition. As an example, PC1 specification dictates print substrate (PS1), coloration description (CD1), and two screening specifications (periodic and nonperiodic).

4. TVI: TVI aims are different for different grades of paper. For a given paper grade, the same TVI curves are specified for all four process colors.

5. Tolerances: Table 4.4 specifies colorimetric tolerances of process color solids of all printing conditions (PC1–PC8). Deviation tolerance (5 ΔE^*_{ab}) is the permissive color difference between the OK print and the aims. The OK sheet must pass all normative requirements. Production variation tolerance is the permissive color difference between multiple production samples and the OK print. Specifically, for at least 68% of the prints, the color differences between a production print and the OK print shall not exceed the specified amounts (the "7 out of 10" rule). Notice that (1) both ΔE^*_{ab} (normative) and ΔE_{00} (informative) are specified, and (2) except for black, ΔE_{00} is a bigger color difference unit than ΔE^*_{ab}.

Table 4.4. ISO 12647-2 (2013b) lithographic tolerance specifications.

Color	Deviation		Variation		
	ΔE^*_{ab}	ΔE_{00}	ΔE^*_{ab}	ΔE_{00}	ΔH^*
K	5	5	4	4	3
C	5	3.5	4	2.8	3
M	5	3.5	4	2.8	3
Y	5	3.5	4	3.5	3

4.12. ISO 12647-6: Process Control for Flexographic Printing

ISO 12647-6 (2012b), different from ISO 12647-2 (2013a), recognizes a specific reference printing condition (characterization data set) as printing aims. The standard is applicable to publication flexographic printing and packaging flexographic printing, including labels, boxes, and flexible packages.

Both films and digital data are acceptable as input material for flexographic printing. This input material must be accompanied by a proof prepared in accordance with ISO 12647-7 hard-copy contract proof (ISO, 2015b) or ISO 14861 soft display proof (ISO, 2013b).

The printer is responsible for demonstrating a consistent reproducible printing process by using the appropriate anilox rollers, printing forms, inks, and electronic data manipulation (e.g., ISO/TS 10128) to achieve final printed images that colorimetrically match the specified characterization data. When the substrate color falls outside the specified ranges, the SCCA (substrate-corrected colorimetric aims) method shall be used to adjust the characterization data to obtain the adjusted process control aims.

The printing aim is to match a characterization data set. Thus, no specific TVI curves are specified. Both deviation tolerance and variation tolerance are specified for process color solids and spot color solids (Table 4.5). Notice that the hue angle difference (Δh) is used as a deviation tolerance metric. The testing method for the variation conformity is the same as ISO 12647-2, that is, 68% of the production samples cannot exceed the specified tolerances.

Table 4.5. ISO 12647-6 (2012b) flexographic tolerance specifications.

	Black	Cyan	Magenta	Yellow	Spot color
Deviation tolerance	$5\,\Delta L^*$ $3\,\Delta C^*$	$6\,\Delta h_{ab}$	$6\,\Delta h_{ab}$	$6\,\Delta h_{ab}$	$8\,\Delta h_{ab}$
Variation tolerance	$3\,\Delta E_{00}$	$2\,\Delta E_{00}$	$2\,\Delta E_{00}$	$2\,\Delta E_{00}$	$1.5\,\Delta E_{00}$

4.13. ISO 12647-7: Proofing Processes Working Directly from Digital Data

ISO 12647-7 (ISO, 2015b) assumes that by matching to the same characterization data set, the proof will simulate visual characteristics of the production print. The simulation must satisfy the following technical requirements:

1. Digital data is in the form of PDF/X file.

2. Digital proofing substrates, which seldom match the production substrates, should have similar gloss, fluorescence, and color, with the L^* slightly higher than the production stock.

3. The three-tier digital control strip (Figure 4.2) and the color characterization target (Figure 4.3) included in the proof are used to verify color conformance.

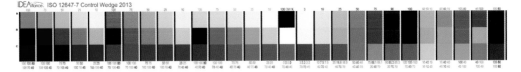

Figure 4.2.
ISO 12647-7 three-tier digital control strip. (Image courtesy of Idealliance.)

4. The process color solids shall agree with the aim values of the printing condition to be simulated within 3 ΔE_{00}. The hue difference (Δh) for CMY solids shall not exceed 2.5°.

5. Additional digital proofing tolerances for control patches are shown in Table 4.6.

Table 4.6. ISO 12647-7 (2015d) additional digital proofing tolerance specifications.

Control patch description	Unit	Tolerance
All patches of the digital control bar except spot color ink patches	Maximum ΔE_{00} Average ΔE_{00}	5.0 2.5
A CMY overprint scale replicating the neutral scale with a minimum of five patches	Maximum ΔC_h Average ΔC_h	3.5 2.0
All patches of ISO 12642-2	Average ΔE_{00} 95th percentile ΔE_{00}	2.5 5.0
All spot color ink solid patches specified in the digital control bar	Maximum ΔE_{00}	2.5

Annex D of ISO 12647-7 provides a procedure to visually assess proof–print color match. It assumes that there are many observers to choose from, and large variance exists among observers. Thus, the first step is to conduct color vision tests (Ishihara's test for color blindness and Farnsworth-Munsell 100 hue test) to screen observers. The second step is to use a training set (press print and marked proofs, indicating passed, just passed, just failed, and failed) to gauge how color differences should be judged. The third step is to use press prints and unmarked proofs to select the observers who tend to form consensus with other observers.

4.14. ISO 12647-8: Validation Print Processes Working Directly from Digital Data

A validation print is intended to promote color consistency at multiple sites and in early stages of the design and print production workflow (ISO, 2012c). As shown in Table 4.7, ISO 12647-8 uses ΔE^*_{ab} to define color difference requirements. The requirements for validation prints are less stringent than the requirements for contract proofs.

Table 4.7. ISO 12647-8 (2012c) validation print tolerance specifications.

Control patch description	Unit	Tolerance
All patches of the digital control bar	Maximum ΔE^*_{ab} Average ΔE^*_{ab}	8 3
C, M, Y, R, G, B solids	Maximum ΔH	4
Neutral scale of the digital control bar	Average ΔC_h	2.5
Selected surface gamut patches of ISO 12642-2	Average ΔE^*_{ab}	4
All patches of ISO 12642-2	Average ΔE^*_{ab} 95 % percentile ΔE^*_{ab}	3 6

4.15. ISO/PAS 15339: Printing from Digital Data across Multiple Technologies

ISO/PAS 15339 is a two-part printing standard applicable to multiple technologies printing from digital data. Part 1 of the standard focuses on principles (CRPC; ISO, 2015c); and part 2 of the standard specifies characterized reference printing conditions (ISO, 2015d).

Based on the color-management principle, ISO/PAS 15339-1 uses color characterization data (CRPC) to define the relationship between CMYK (input data) and printed or proofed color. ISO/PAS 15339-1 provides the SCCA method to "adjust" CRPC for paper color changes. Printed colors are measured in the M1 measurement conditions (ISO, 2009b) and viewed in the standard viewing conditions (ISO, 2009a).

To ensure printing conformity to CRPC, ISO/PAS 15339-1 requires the use of the ISO 12642-2 target, as shown in Figure 4.3, as the input (ISO, 2005a). The printing process can be calibrated per ISO/TS 10128. Printed colors are determined by paper, ink, printing conditions, and measurement conditions.

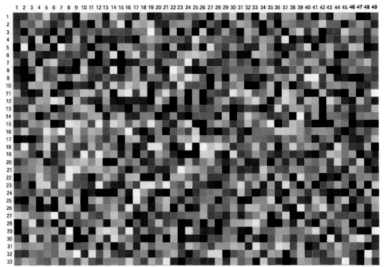

Figure 4.3.
A randomized
version of the ISO
12642-2 target.
(Reproduced with
permission from
ANSI on behalf of ISO.
All rights reserved.)

ISO 12642-2:2005

Color deviation is the color difference between the initial press sheets, containing the ISO 12642-2 target plus process control patches. The 95th percentile ΔE_{00} between the ISO 12642-2 measurements and the substrate-corrected colorimetric aims (SCCA) is compared with the specified tolerances for conformity decision. Conformity fails if any one of the ΔE_{00} values from the process control patches plus the 95th percentile ΔE_{00} exceeds the specified tolerances.

ISO/PAS 15339-1 Aims: ISO/PAS 15339-1 specifies one of the seven CRPCs as printing aims. The seven CRPCs cover a range of substrates, which results in different color gamut sizes (Figure 4.4). The larger the color gamut is, the more expensive the substrate will be. Although differing in gamut volume, CRPC1 to CRPC7 have common hue angles of the primaries. CRPC1 to CRPC7 also have similar highlight-to-midtone contrast, and gray reproduction characteristics in relation to predefined neutrals.

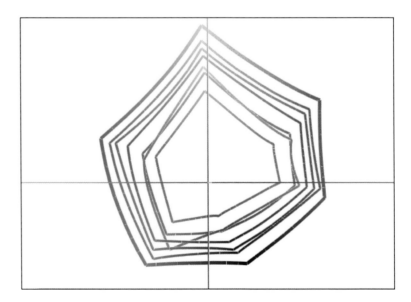

Figure 4.4.
Color gamut of
CRPC1 (innermost)
and CRPC7
(outermost).

ISO/PAS 15339-1 Tolerances: ISO/PAS 15339-1 specifies three types of tolerance: (1) deviation tolerance is the ability to match the CRPC aims; (2) spatial variation tolerance is the within-sheet color variation; and (3) production variation tolerance is the within-run color variation. Sections 9.6–9.11 discuss the use of ISO/PAS 15339-1 and three case studies to achieve proof-print match.

4.16. Tolerance Metrics: ΔE^*_{ab} and ΔE_{00}

ISO/TC 130 is the standardization body in the printing industry. When revising color tolerances, many issues—metric, magnitude, precision, sampling, test method, normative or informative, and instrumentation—have to be reviewed, debated, and decided by consensus. These factors are discussed below:

Metric and magnitude: Color deviation and color variation tolerances are specified in ΔE^*_{ab} metric since the 1996 version of ISO 12647-2. There are studies indicating that the ΔE_{00} metric shows higher correlation with perceived color difference than ΔE^*_{ab} metric. During its 2010 plenary meeting in Sao Paulo, Brazil, TC 130 resolved to replace ΔE^*_{ab} with ΔE_{00} for all new ISO/TC 130 standards and revisions of existing standards (ISO, 2010a).

Replacing ΔE^*_{ab} metric by ΔE_{00} metric turned out to be nontrivial. To elaborate, points on the circumference of a circle have equal distances to its center. This is similar to colors with equal ΔE^*_{ab} to their aim points; they do not map into a circle, but an ellipse. Other concerns to replace ΔE^*_{ab} metric by ΔE_{00} metric include "prints which previously are acceptable may be rejected," "prints which are not acceptable visually become numerically within specification," etc. One logical approach is to use a printing database to maximize the agreement between ΔE_{00} metric and ΔE^*_{ab} *metric* among conforming jobs and nonconforming jobs. This may result in unequal tolerances among CMYK solids, and unequal tolerances may be too complex for the market to embrace (Chung and Chen, 2011c).

Precision: Tolerance should include the level of precision or the number of significant figures required for conformity assessment. For example, a tolerance of 3, with one significant figure, will accept measurements up to 3.4 (3.4 will be rounded to 3); and a tolerance of 3.5, with two significant figures, will accept measurements up to 3.54 (3.54 will be rounded to 3.5).

Sampling and test method: Technical standards address sampling to verify the reproducibility of the test method. Conformity standards address sampling to assess conformity. While samples must be randomly selected, it is not clear whether the sample size can be kept the same for two very different purposes.

Normative or informative: There are two undesirable ways to set color tolerances (Berns, 2000): (1) set the tolerance according to perceptibility thresholds, and (2) make the tolerance as tight as possible. A reasonable solution in ISO standards is to use the terms *shall* and *should* when setting tolerance specifications. *Shall* is normative and it means "must comply" to a more relaxed tolerance; *should* is informative and it means "nice to comply" to a more stringent tolerance. For example, spot color tolerance shall be 3.0 ΔE_{00} and should be 2.0 ΔE_{00}.

4.17. ISO 20654 (2016): Measurement and Calculation of Spot Color Tonal Value

Spot colors are non-CMYK colors. Spot color solids are used widely in packaging printing. Process control parameters for spot color solids (ΔE_{00}, hue angle, etc.) are covered in ISO 12647-6 Flexographic printing. But the need for process control of spot color tints became necessary as more and more spot color tints are being printed in packaging product designs. Without a clear definition of tonal value for spot color inks, design and prepress software (e.g., Adobe CS applications) would have limited success when visualizing and communicating spot color tints from design, prepress, to production.

As discussed in chapter 1, "Densitometry," process color tints are modeled by the Murray-Davies equation. An immediate question is: "Is there an advantage to calculating spot color tonal value using the Murray-Davies equation?" A number of studies were conducted by the TC 130/WG3 experts, and they concluded that the Murray-Davies method does not work well with spot color tints. In many cases, it produced a tone scale that was far from being perceptually uniform.

A number of spot color tone value (SCTV) models were proposed and studied. By consensus, ISO/TC 130 selected Eq. 4.1 to define SCTV, because it can be calculated from either the measured spectral reflectance values or from the colorimetric values. In other words, the SCTV is defined as a substrate-relative metric and normalized between substrate (0%) and spot ink solid (100%).

$$SCTV = 100\times\sqrt{\frac{\left(V_{xt}-V_{xp}\right)^2+\left(V_{yt}-V_{yp}\right)^2+\left(V_{zt}-V_{zp}\right)^2}{\left(V_{xs}-V_{xp}\right)^2+\left(V_{ys}-V_{yp}\right)^2+\left(V_{zs}-V_{zp}\right)^2}} \qquad \text{Eq. 4.1}$$

where V_{xs}, V_{ys}, and V_{zs} are values of the spot color solid; V_{xp}, V_{yp}, and V_{zp} are values of the substrate; and V_{xt}, V_{yt}, and V_{zt} are values of the spot color tint.

SCTV produces approximately uniform visual spacing of the tones between the unprinted substrate and the solid ink coverage. It is a new tool to analyze halftone reproduction in which spot color inks are used for brand color and packaging printing. It is expected that (1) SCTV calculation will be included in color-measurement hardware and process control software, (2) use cases will be reported by early adopters, and (3) the SCTV metric will be used as a normative or informative requirement in other ISO standards.

4.18. Chapter Summary

Digital data exchange marked the beginning of graphic arts technology standards development in 1982. As soon as the digital data exchange standards were developed, it became apparent that the meaning of the image data must be defined and controlled. From this point on, the relationship between digital data and printed color became the focus of graphic arts technology standard development.

Printing standards help align quality expectations for print buyers and print producers. Printing standards turn subjective print-quality judgments into measurable and objective criteria.

The relationship between instrumental color difference and visual color difference also became the focus of graphic arts technology standards development. Understandably, ΔE_{00} is a better estimate of visual color difference than ΔE^*_{ab}. So far, ISO 12647-2 still specifies ΔE^*_{ab} as a normative metric and ΔE_{00} as an informative metric.

4.19. Multiple-Choice and Essay Questions

1. _____ contains normative requirements and must be approved by two-thirds of the P-members, and that not more than one-quarter of the total number of votes cast are negative.
A. IS
B. TS
C. TR
D. PAS

2. Which of the following is *false* in relation to the nature of industry standards?
A. Mandatory
B. Address common needs
C. Voluntary
D. Practical and achievable

3. Graphic arts technology standards, e.g., ISO 13655, ISO 3664, are _____ whereby vendors can create standard-compliant products for the user community.
A. process capability
B. specifications
C. needs and wants
D. conformity requirements

4. ISO/TC 130/WG1 is responsible for developing _____.
A. terminology
B. digital data exchange
C. process control
D. safety

5. When a standard undergoes its periodic review, it may be _____.
A. Reaffirmed
B. Revised
C. Withdrawn
D. All of the above

6. The ISO 12647-2 standard specifies color of the ink sets for process color printing by _____.
A. CIEXYZ
B. CIEYxy
C. CIELAB
D. CIE/CMYK

7. The advantage of standardizing printing plate sizes is _____.
A. reduced inventory
B. faster press makeready
C. wider color gamut printing
D. finer resolution

8. ISO 12647-6 Flexo, differing from ISO 12647-2 Offset Litho, recognizes _____ as printing aims.
A. characterization data set
B. solid coloration
C. TVI
D. gray balance

9. SWOP, Specifications for Web Offset Publication, defines the desired level of quality for the _____ printing industry.
A. commercial
B. publication
C. packaging
D. All of the above

10. The primary cause of color gamut differences in CRPC1–CRPC7 is _____.
A. ink
B. paper
C. press
D. printing variation

11. Elaborate on how ISO standards use the terms *shall* and *should* differently in setting tolerance specifications.

12. How is production variation conformity specified in ISO 12647-2?

5   Printing Conformity Assessment

Printing standards specify aims and tolerances. Metrology enables printing by numbers. Printing conformity brings standards and metrology together to help build trust between print buyers and printers. This chapter covers conformity assessment, conformity assessment actions, printing conformity standards development activities, and printing certification activities around the world.

5.1.   Conformity Assessment

Conformity assessment means checking whether products, processes, systems, and personnel measure up to specified requirements. Conformity assessment varies in its scope and applies to different areas of the operations.

In today's society, product quality, safety, and environmental impact are of key concerns to manufacturers and consumers. Conformity assessment activities include testing, inspection, auditing, and attestation. For example, the design, manufacturing, and distribution of TV sets encompass many conformity assessment activities. To elaborate, testing and inspection require the use of metrology to examine products, processes, and personnel; auditing requires sampling, testing, and the use of applicable standards.

5.2.   Why Conformity Assessment?

Conformity assessment is a supply-side (producer) strategy, because conformance to standards ensures quality. By preventing problems and enforcing best practices, conformity assessment enables producers to be more competitive. By encouraging standards-compliant certification, conformity assessment helps promote a company's reputation and provides access to world markets. When the perceived risk of producing defective products is high (e.g., food safety), the demand for conformity assessment is also high. Although conformity assessment takes time and adds cost, it helps reduce the risk of producing defective products. When process control is defect-prevention based, the savings may easily pay for the cost of conformity assessment.

Conformity assessment is also a demand-side (purchaser) strategy.

This is because conformity assessment provides the means for testing the compliance of products in accordance with relevant standards. By removing the need for buyers to verify directly whether the products they acquire meet specifications, conformity assessment allows buyers to make their buying decisions on the basis of certificates issued, and thereby eases the burden in managing the supply chain.

5.3. ISO/CASCO, the Conformity Assessment Authority

CASCO, the conformity assessment policy development committee, is the international authority on conformity assessment. It develops conformity assessment principles and guidelines and oversees the deployment of these policies in ISO TCs. However, CASCO is not involved in conformity assessment activities, that is, writing schemes, training consultants, performing audits, issuing certificates, and so on.

CASCO believes that metrology, standardization, and conformity assessment are the three components of quality infrastructure. Furthermore, CASCO considers "one standard, one test, one conformity, accepted everywhere" to be its ultimate goal. Perhaps this is an idealistic view of conformity assessment activities, because (1) technical standards differ in scopes, test methods, and requirements; and (2) conformity assessment requirements differ from region to region.

At its 2010 plenary meeting in Sao Paulo, ISO/TC 130 resolved to initiate work, at Stage 0, to create standards documents under the title: *Graphic Technology—Printing Conformity Assessment* (ISO, 2010a). This work is to be done in a new Working Group, WG13. Thus, the interaction between technical standards activities and conformity assessment standards activities may be illustrated in Figure 5.1. Under CASCO's stewardship, ISO/TC 130/WG13 develops printing conformity guidelines for scheme writers and promotes conformity assessment activities around the world.

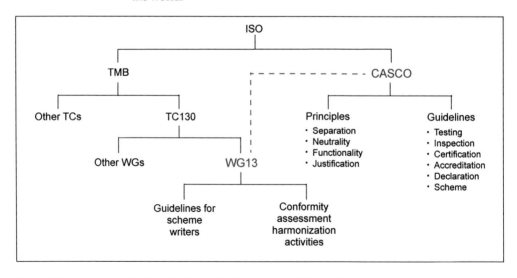

Figure 5.1. Interaction between technical standards and conformity assessment standards.

5.4. Conformity Assessment Principles

ISO/CASCO principles and guidelines enable various parties, for example, ISO/TC 130/WG13, interested in conformity assessment to develop sector-specific documents. Among others, four general principles of conformity assessment are discussed here (ISO, 2010b).

1. **Technical standards should not contain conformity assessment activities requirements.**
While technical standards cover sampling and testing methods related to the specified characteristics, they should not dictate conformity assessment activities, for example, who should perform the assessment.

2. **Neutrality toward parties performing conformity assessment activities.**
All documents containing requirements for products, processes, and personnel should be written such that conformity can be assessed by a manufacturer or supplier (first-party assessment), a user or purchaser (second-party assessment), or an independent body (third-party assessment).

3. **Conformity assessment schemes should be functional.**
ISO/CASCO (ISO, 2010b) specifies that all product certification schemes involve testing and assessing product characteristics, but these schemes may vary in their assessment scopes. When writing a conformity assessment scheme, consider the following approach:
a. Define workflow specifications and resources required.
b. Determine test method, sampling, measurement, aims, and tolerances.
c. Specify the auditing process, for example, who is involved.
d. Report the outcome (pass/fail) of the conformity assessment and issue a statement of conformity, when passed.
e. Consider surveillance, that is, further conformity assessment activities before recertification.

4. **Prepare a justification study before developing conformity assessment documents.**
ISO/CASCO does not encourage the unnecessary proliferation of sector documents. If there is a genuine need by a sector for such a document, a justification study is required before the development process begins.

5.5. Conformity Assessment Guidelines

Conformity assessment activities include, but are not limited to, testing, inspection, certification, accreditation, declaration, and scheme. ISO/CASCO provides guidelines for these activities (MacCurtain, 2011).

1. **Guidelines on Testing**
Testing is used to make decisions on the performance of the product or process, which is tested against a specified set of criteria. Testing provides the basis for product certification.

2. **Guidelines on Inspection**
Inspection is the examination of a product design, product, or process to determine its conformity with specific requirements. Inspection covers a range of workflow procedures, and reports on such parameters as quality, fitness for use, and continuing safety in operation. In the graphic arts industry, inspection encompasses file reception, proofing, and printing in a color-managed workflow. The overall aim of inspection is to reduce the risk of producing defective proofs and defective press sheets.

3. Guidelines on Certification

Certification is the third-party confirmation of certain characteristics of a process. It is the result of an audit process, not self-examination. Certifications are issued by certification bodies who must be creditable, independent, and unbiased.

Certification takes time, costs money, and runs the risk of nonconformity, that is, failing the audit. In addition, different certification schemes specify different standards and conformity assessment activities. Thus, certification is both a business issue and a standardization issue.

4. Guidelines on Accreditation

Accreditation is the third-party attestation related to the competence of certification bodies, including testing laboratories, in carrying out specific conformity assessment activities. In this case, it is the testing laboratories or certification bodies that may be seeking formal recognition from an accreditation council, that is, a member of the International Accreditation Forum (IAF) Multilateral Recognition Arrangement (MLA), regarding their competency and independence.

A certification body may choose to be accredited according to ISO/IEC 17011, *Conformity Assessment—General Requirements for Accrediting Conformity Assessment Bodies* (ISO, 2005b). A testing laboratory may choose to be accredited according to ISO/IEC 17025, *General Requirements for the Competence of Testing and Calibration Laboratories* (ISO, 2005c).

5. Guidelines on Declaration

Declaration is the first-party attestation of conformity assessment. Suppliers commonly use declaration to claim product conformity in the markets. In the graphic arts industry, companies like X-Rite and gti provide declarations, also known as certificates of analysis (CoA) or certificates of conformance (CoC), on their color-measurement instruments and graphic arts viewing booths. A certified printing company can also issue compliant claims relating to specific printed products.

6. Guidelines on Schemes

A scheme is a set of requirements, rules, and procedures that apply to specified products or processes. A scheme owner is a person or an organization responsible for developing and maintaining a specific certification scheme. Scheme owners, institutional or private, specify schemes and promote them in the marketplace. The market decides the fate a scheme.

According to ISO 17067, *Conformity Assessment—Fundamentals of Product Certification and Guidelines for Product Certification Schemes* (ISO, 2013c), product certification schemes may vary in their scopes of conformity assessment activities. As shown in Table 5.1, a Type 1a scheme specifies calibration conformity only, and it does not cover production conformity; a Type 3 scheme specifies calibration, production, and surveillance conformity; and a Type 5 scheme covers calibration, production, surveillance, and a quality-management system (QMS) component.

Table 5.1. Scope of certification schemes, per ISO 17067.

	Calibration	**Production**	**Surveillance**	**QMS**
Type 1a	X			
Type 3	X	X		
Type 5	X	X	X	X

To sum up, certification schemes vary in scopes, sampling requirements, and testing methods. Type 1 schemes only assess calibration deviation using initial samples. Type 3 schemes assess both production deviation and production variation using multiple samples, pulled randomly from a production line.

ISO/TC 130 standards (e.g., ISO 12647-2 [ISO, 2013a] and ISO/TS 15311-1 [ISO, 2018]), define sampling requirements differently. We will discuss this topic in chapter 9, "Printing Standards in a Changing Industry."

5.6. Examples of Printing Certification Schemes

In the graphic arts industry, printing certification is both a technical issue and a business issue. Printing certification schemes vary in their scopes and differ in pass/fail criteria. Below are three examples of printing certification schemes: G7, PSO, and PSA.

1. G7 Scheme

Idealliance operates G7 in three tiers: (a) *G7 grayscale*, the first tier, focuses on achieving gray and tone reproduction conformity, including the use of nonstandard inks and substrates. G7 grayscale specifies the submission of a single sample of print and proof that is assessed for calibration deviation only; (b) *G7 targeted* is the next tier. In addition to achieving G7 grayscale specifications, G7 targeted must conform to the substrate color and CMYRGB solid coloration of a G7 color space; and (c) *G7 colorspace* is the most stringent level of compliance. In addition to achieving G7 targeted specifications, G7 colorspace must conform to the specified color characterization data set (Idealliance, 2018). A G7 consultant is required as a part of the auditing process. Recertification is annual, and there is no surveillance required.

All three tiers of the G7 scheme represent an ISO/IEC 17067 Type 1a (calibration only) scheme. G7 does not assess production deviation or production variation conformity.

2. Process Standard Offset (PSO) Scheme

bvdm is the PSO scheme owner. Fogra is the PSO certification body. The PSO scheme is based on ISO 12647-2 standard (ISO, 2013a). PSO, an ISO 17067 Type 3 scheme, requires the submission of single samples of print and proof for calibration deviation conformity assessment. In addition, it requires multiple (20) samples of prints for production variation conformity assessment. PSO was introduced to the European market in 2004.

PSO defines calibration deviation according to ISO 12647-2, that is, 5 ΔE^*_{ab} as the permissive color difference between CMYK solids of the OK print and the aims. However, PSO defines production variation between multiple production samples and the OK print (not the production center).

3. Printing Standards Audit (PSA) Scheme

RIT is the PSA scheme owner. PSA, an ISO 17067 Type 3 scheme, focuses on data set conformance with substrate correction (SCCA) to reconcile the difference between the reference paper and the printing paper. SCCA addresses the print buyer's paper preference, thus increasing its real-world applicability. Printers are responsible for press calibration and process control.

PSA requires the submission of single samples of print and proof, containing the ISO 12642-2 color characterization target, for calibration deviation assessment. PSA requires the submission of multiple (20) samples of prints containing CMYK solids, CMYK 50% tints, and the C50M40Y40 tint for production variation assessment.

5.7. ISO/TC 130/WG13 Printing Certification Activities

ISO/TC 130/WG13, Printing Conformity Requirements, was formed in 2010. WG13 membership is made up of the global experts from ISO/TC 130 member bodies. These experts are involved in conformity assessment activities, as well as in technical standards development activities. The goal of WG13 is to harmonize printing conformity activities internationally.

A WG13 justification study was submitted to ISO/CASCO in 2012. The outcome of the study indicated that (1) WG13 cannot write certification schemes; (2) WG13 cannot develop general principles of conformity assessment, and (3) WG13 can develop guidelines for printing certification scheme writers.

WG13 activities include the development of the following three documents: (1) ISO 19301, scheme guidelines that address color quality management; (2) ISO 19302, scheme guidelines that evaluate tone and color reproduction requirements for any printing process; and (3) ISO/TS 19303-1, scheme guidelines that address conformity assessment of packaging printing color reproduction. The three WG13 documents are discussed in more detail below:

5.8. ISO 19301: *Graphic Technology—Guidelines for Schema Writers—Template for Colour Quality Management*

ISO 19301 (2017a) provides guidelines that can be used as a blueprint for ISO 17067 Type 5 sector-specific schemes. This guideline is based on the requirements of ISO 9001 (2008) with a scope limited to tone and color reproduction.

Site locations of the organization to be certified, including outsourced sites, must be specified. Site locations may be included only if the color-quality system applies at a particular site, and an audit product test has been successfully conducted at that site.

The guidelines do not specify tone and color reproduction requirements, because there are a number of ISO/TC130 standards (e.g., ISO 12647 series, ISO/PAS 15339 series, ISO 15311) that may apply. Instead, the organization to be certified specifies the applicable ISO standards (aims, tolerances), production process (analog printing, digital printing), and custom printing conditions (if applicable).

The guidelines for a QMS (quality-management system) scheme should focus on the following:

1. The context of the organization, for example, who, what is involved, and why.
2. Leadership, including the color-quality policy statement.
3. Planning for what is needed, for example, objectives, resources, timetable, to make the system work.
4. Support, for example, control of system documents, training, etc.
5. Operation, including how measurement and calibration are carried out.
6. Performance evaluation, including self-assessment of the printed products and QMS.
7. Improvement on not just what is found to be wrong, but also the system itself to make it more effective.

5.9. ISO 19302: *Graphic Technology—Colour Conformity of Printed Products*

ISO 19302 develops ISO 17067 Type 3 scheme requirements to evaluate tone and color reproduction for any printing process (ISO, 2017b). This standard defines three stages of a color-managed workflow: color definition, color reproduction, and color conformity. It specifies applicable ISO standards at each stage of the workflow, including device calibration, process control, and test conditions for conformity assessment.

The organization to be certified, and the certification body, must agree to the following before the conformity assessment audit: (1) specific workflow stages; (2) applicable standards, including aims and tolerances, for device calibration and printing-process control; (3) sampling; (4) audit logistics; and (5) conformity scoring (pass/fail) criteria.

In the color definition stage of the workflow, digital files, including the reference printing condition and spot color specifications, are specified and preflighted according to ISO 15930-7 PDF/X-4 specifications (ISO, 2007b).

In the color reproduction stage of the workflow, which begins with prepress, digital files should be delivered with digital hard-copy proofs, per ISO 12647-7, that match the intended printing condition, including the influence of the printing stock (ISO, 2015b).

The print service provider is responsible for device calibration, per ISO/TS 10128 (ISO, 2015a). The print service provider is also responsible for printing-process control activities. Test methods for process control are specified by the ISO 12647 series. Both calibration deviation tolerances and production variation tolerances are specified. Test methods for printing to the color characterization data set are specified according to ISO/PAS 15339-1 (ISO, 2015c).

Color conformity is viewed as the last stage of the color-managed workflow. Two scoring schemes, one based on ISO 12647-2 (conformity to process control parameters) and the other based on ISO/PAS 15339 and CGATS TR 016 (conformity to color characterization data set; CGATS, 2014), are included in the annex of the standard.

This standard provides printers, suppliers, and customers, as well as independent bodies, with guidelines that will allow them to assess whether a printing workflow demonstrates color conformity.

5.10. ISO/TS 19303-1: *Graphic Technology—Certification Scheme Guidelines*, Part 1, *Packaging Printing* (ISO, 2017c)

ISO/TS 19303-1 specifies certification scheme guidelines for packaging printing workflows, that is, CMYK, CMYK with spot color, non-CMYK, spot color only, and multicolor printing. It also provides a collection of international standards, including aims, tolerances, and test methods, applicable at each stage of packaging printing workflow.

By defining a reference packaging printing workflow, ISO/TS 19303-1 provides technical and conformity assessment guidelines to scheme owners. Supply-chain communication requirements and process-dependent checklists for flexography, gravure, offset, digital inkjet, and digital toner are also included in this document.

CoA (certificate of analysis) and CoC (certificate of conformance) are first-party declarations provided by material providers in the supply chain, including inks, substrates, laminates, and finishing. These documents should reference to ASTM (American Society for Testing and Materials), ISO, or industry best practices.

ISO/TS 19303-1 provides a framework that scheme owners (e.g., FIRST Company Certification [FTA, 2019]) can follow, thus enabling mutual recognition of the certifications of other bodies, as well as allowing international trade organizations to identify comparable competencies on a worldwide basis.

5.11. Two ISO Printing Aims: ISO 12647-2 and ISO/PAS 15339

There are two ISO printing standards applicable to printing conformity schemes: (1) ISO 12647-2 (ISO, 2013a) and (2) ISO/PAS 15339 (ISO, 2015c). They differ in test target, sampling, test method, and pass/fail criteria.

1. ISO 12647-2 aim points and tolerances

To assess calibration deviation, ISO 12647-2 specifies CMYK solids and tints as the input. The deviation tolerance is the permissive difference (ΔE^*_{ab} of solids, ΔTVI of tints, MTS) between measurements from the OK sheet and the aim points (Figure 5.2).

To assess production variation, ISO 12647-2 specifies the variation tolerance as the permissive difference (ΔE^*_{ab} of solids, ΔTVI of tints, MTS) between the sample measurements (15–20) taken at random and the OK sheet (Figure 5.3). The fraction required for conformity is 68%, or the "7 out of 10" rule.

When replacing the aim points with the OK sheet, there is no information regarding run-to-run color consistency. Some acceptable production samples may be twice the tolerance from the specified aims.

Left: **Figure 5.2.**
ISO 12647-2 deviation tolerance.

Right: **Figure 5.3.**
ISO 12647-2 variation tolerance.

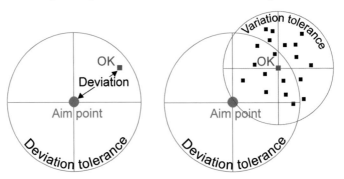

2. ISO/PAS 15339-1 aim points and tolerances

To assess calibration deviation, ISO/PAS 15339-1 specifies the color characterization target, containing 1617 color patches, as the input. The deviation conformity is the permissive difference (95th percentile ΔE_{00}) between the color characterization target measurements of the initial sheets and the aim point data set (Figure 5.4). In this example, the 95th percentile ΔE_{00} is 4.4 and it passes Level III CGATS TR 016 (2014) tolerance.

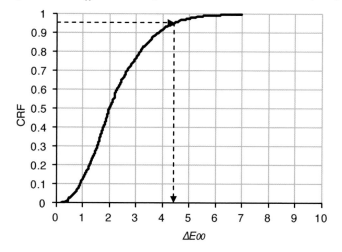

Figure 5.4.
ISO/PAS 15339-1
calibration deviation
assessment.

To assess production variation, ISO/PAS 15339-1 does not explicitly specify tolerances, but addresses tolerance schemes as an annex which is similar to CGATS TR 016. To elaborate, CGATS TR 016 specifies CMYK solids, CMYK 50% tints, and a near-neutral triplet (C50M40Y40) as the input to assess production variation. The variation conformity is the permissive difference (70th percentile ΔE_{00}) between the sample measurements (15-20) and the aim points. As shown in Figure 5.5, production variation of the CMYK solids and 50% tints are displayed as solid lines and dash lines respectively; and the production variation of the near-neutral triplet is shown in solid gray line. In this example, the near-neutral triplet has the largest color difference (3.4 ΔE_{00}) among all nine color patches. The production variation assessment passes Level III CGATS TR 016 (2014) tolerance.

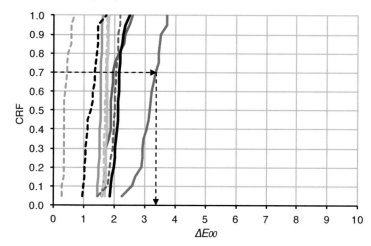

Figure 5.5.
ISO/PAS 15339-1
production variation
assessment.

5.12. Institutional Certification Schemes

There were information-sharing sessions on certification activities at ISO/TC 130/WG13 meetings. Some observations of certification activities, country by country, are described below. The statistics collected and issues identified are incidental and will change over time.

Brazil: The Brazilian certification body, ABTG, develops certification schemes and provides training for security printing and newspaper sectors. There are 22 certified printers. The commercial printing certification scheme is according to ISO 12647-2. Brazilian experts commented that the certified companies are typically big offset printers motivated by market recognition.

China: The Chinese printing industry does not have its own certification body and certification scheme. Many printers in Hong Kong and southern China export printing to the U.S. and European markets. There are more than 200 certified printers in China. Most of them are G7 certified and a small number of them are PSA, Fogra PSO, or Ugra PSO certified. Chinese experts observed that certified printers are motivated by customer requirements and operational efficiency.

France: The French printing industry does not have its own certification body or certification scheme. Forty-three printers in France are Ugra PSO certified. The French printing industry association, UNIC, launched its ISO 12647 standardization initiative in 2013. Fifty French printers were selected to participate, and 12 completed the training objectives. French experts reported that there was a 30% reduction in the number of printers in Europe in the past 10 years. Printers both with and without certification had closed their businesses. They believe that automation is key to a printer's survival.

Germany: bvdm and Fogra jointly developed a PSO scheme in 2004. PSO is targeted to companies of different sizes as long as they have four-color printing presses. The German printing industry is well informed about the value of certification. There are more than 200 PSO-certified printers in Germany, compared with more than 100 PSO-certified printers elsewhere around the world. German experts believe that adhering to one ISO standard is a way of harmonizing printing certification worldwide.

Italy: CertiPrint and cmyQ are the certification schemes in Italy. There are 10 CertiPrint- and cmyQ-certified printers, plus 8 Fogra and Ugra PSO-certified printers in Italy. Italian experts remarked that there are more than 300 Italian printers working with the standards without being certified, and that certification was perceived as having marketing value only.

Japan: The Japanese certification body, JPMA, issued 348 certifications in Japan. Among them, 164 offset printers were certified according to the ISO 12647-2 standard (ISO, 2013b). Thirty-eight printing companies were certified for conformity to the JapanColor data set. In addition, 74 certifications were awarded to proofing system vendors according to ISO 12647-7 (ISO, 2015b); and 72 proofing process management certifications were awarded to prepress companies. Japanese experts observed that the number of certified printers, systems, and design/prepress houses has increased since 2012.

Netherlands: SCGM is the certification scheme in the Netherlands and Belgium. There are 37 SCGM-certified printers. The number of certified printers has declined since 2009. Reasons for the decline included bankruptcy/merger of certified companies, certified printers choosing not to renew, and printers failing the recertification process. The experts from the Netherlands commented that misinformed experts and confusing documents were causes for the decline.

Sweden: CGP, Certified Graphic Arts Production, is the certification scheme in Sweden. Sixteen Swedish printers were certified according to the ISO 12647-2 standard. Swedish experts reported that the total number of printers in Sweden decreased. In addition, they believe that a single standard certification scheme is better than many certification schemes to serve the world markets.

Switzerland: Ugra PSO is the Swiss certification scheme. In addition to the 38 Ugra PSO-certified printers in Switzerland, there are 55 Ugra PSO-certified printers around the world, including printers in Europe and Asia. Swiss experts believe that the force of the markets in choosing certification schemes is greater than the force of standardization bodies in harmonizing certification activities. Furthermore, they believe that educating print buyers is the most effective way to promote and increase certification in the printing industry.

United Kingdom: Printed & Media Certification (PMC) provides certification services. BPiF ISO 12647, a Type 5 scheme, is the certification scheme in the United Kingdom, and comprises calibration, production variation, surveillance, and QMS. There are five BPiF ISO 12647 color quality–management certified printers in the United Kingdom. Many UK printers are certified according to private schemes. British experts commented that 80% of companies failed in their first audits according to the BPiF scheme. Lack of employee training is the most problematic issue.

United States: Idealliance is the G7 scheme owner. RIT is the PSA scheme owner. Idealliance relies on G7 experts to work directly with printers, providing training and disseminating best practices, while keeping the certification schemes simple and affordable. Idealliance also provides training to print buyers and brand owners, because their needs are the greatest motivation for printers to get certified.

5.13. Private Certification Schemes

In addition to institutional schemes, there are private certification schemes around the world. We can categorize these private certification schemes into two classes:

1. Schemes to Manage Print Supply Chains

Graphic Measures International (GMI) certifies the performance of printing and packaging suppliers through print-quality assessment.

GMI-certified printers (more than 200 in China) perform production-run sample measurements to ensure compliance with brand specifications. To help close the loop, GMI monitors results at the retail level through in-store surveillance.

UK-based Mellowcolour certified printers who received training in the implementation of ISO 12647 and the Mellowcolour Print Quality Management System.

2. Schemes to Maximize Technology Utilization

Heidelberg ISO 12647-2 certification enables the printer to prove to its customers that the print quality has achieved the highest standards in color repeatability. The certificate is valid for 24 months with follow-up surveillance after 6, 12, and 18 months.

Pantone-certified printers, offered by X-Rite, are capable of matching Pantone colors consistently, using CMYK and spot colors by analyzing their color-managed workflows from preflight to proofing to ink formulation and finally to process control in the pressroom.

5.14. Chapter Summary

Printing certification schemes should address print buyers' supply-chain management needs and printers' needs to demonstrate their capabilities. The more geographically distributed printing operations are, the more compelling the benefits of printing certification become.

The ISO standard development process requires separation of technical requirements and conformity assessment requirements. This means that ISO/TC 130/WG3 should develop technical standards and ISO/TC 130/WG13 should develop conformity assessment guidelines applicable for the evaluation of tone and color reproduction quality and the evaluation of a color QMS. These conformity assessment guidelines will assist certification bodies and scheme developers. WG13-referenced certification schemes will have comparability in conformity assessment results, and can be mutually recognized internationally as time goes on. The success of these scheme guidelines ultimately depends on how well printing certification scheme owners and certification bodies adopt them in the markets.

ISO 17067 specifies three types of tolerances for conformity assessment: (1) calibration deviation, (2) production deviation, and (3) production variation. ISO 12647-2 and ISO 15339-1 do not specify production deviation explicitly. This will be a topic of further discussion in chapter 9, "Printing Standards in a Changing Industry."

There are two applicable ISO printing standards, that is, ISO 12647-2 and ISO/PAS 15339-1, to enable printing conformity. Unless they can be reconciled, the "one standard, one test method, one conformity, accepted everywhere" goal of ISO/CASCO is unrealistic.

More than 3000 printers have been certified around the world since 2014. Certification activities are motivated by the print buyer's demand, the printer's own desire to be certified, and the printing association's promotion of standards as being valuable. Compared with the number of printing establishments, only a very small percentage of printing companies receive certification.

5.15. Multiple-Choice and Essay Questions

1. _____ is a set of requirements, rules, and procedures that apply to specified product assessment.
A. Inspection
B. Accreditation
C. Surveillance
D. Scheme

2. GMI and MellowColour are examples of _____.
A. institutional certification schemes
B. private certification schemes
C. ISO certification schemes
D. accreditation guidelines

3. _____ focuses on conformance to process control aims, including paper color, solids, and TVI. Both deviation and production variation are assessed.
A. PSO
B. G7
C. PSA
D. All of the above

4. _____ focuses on conformance to process control aims, including neutrality and tone reproduction. Only calibration deviation is assessed.
A. PSO
B. G7
C. PSA
D. All of the above

5. _____ focuses on conformance to a color characterization data set, including SCCA.
A. PSO
B. G7
C. PSA
D. All of the above

6. "One standard, one test, one conformity, accepted everywhere" is the ultimate goal of _____.
A. Idealliance
B. SWOP
C. ISO 12647
D. ISO/CASCO

7. The following TC130 WG13 member bodies developed their own certification schemes, except _____.
A. Brazil
B. China
C. Italy
D. Germany

8. _____ is the confirmation of certain characteristics of a process as the result of an auditing process.
A. Certification
B. Accreditation
C. Justification
D. Scheme

9. Certifications are issued by _____ who are creditable, independent, and unbiased.
A. auditors
B. government
C. certification bodies
D. print buyers

10. A printer in China has been successful in its domestic printing market. What should the printer do strategically to extend its market to the United States?
A. Apply for the PSO certification
B. Apply for the G7 certification
C. Assess its printing quality by itself
D. Institute an aggressive advertising campaign

11. What are the two applicable CMYK printing standards that can be referenced by printing certification schemes?

12. Why is providing training for print buyers and brand owners a key factor in marketing certification schemes?

6   Device Calibration

Device (press or proofer) calibration requires printing a test form, measuring it, and adjusting the device to specified values. It addresses printing accuracy and is a prerequisite to process control. This chapter introduces test forms, process control parameters, and three device calibration methods using CMYK inks, specified in ISO/TS 10128 (ISO, 2015a).

6.1.   Test Form

A test form is a collection of test elements with known device values. Printing a test form enables the visual examination of printed samples. Upon color measurement and analysis, a test form helps characterize the relationship between CMYK values (input) and color (output).

There are two types of test elements in a test form: synthetic and pictorial. We use synthetic test elements in a test form to find out resolution, tonality, and color characteristics of a printing device. Below are examples of synthetic test elements.

6.2.   Synthetic Test Elements

Synthetic test elements, including color control bar, color characterization chart, resolution target, etc., are used to characterize some aspects of a printing device.

1.   Color Control Bar

A color control bar is an important element when implementing printing-process control. A color control bar is composed of an array of patches with known tonal values. Situated in the trim area of the press sheet, a color control bar is primarily used for inking control during press makeready and throughout the pressrun. Typical tonal values include CMYK solids, CMYK midtone tints, two-color RGB overprints, and so on. Figure 6.1 is a color control bar with many features.

The size of each patch should be comparable to the measuring aperture of a scanning or handheld spectro-densitometer; the repeat length of the color control bar should be aligned with the ink keys of a printing press. The characteristics of a color control bar, including screen ruling and dot shape, should be standardized and rasterized at the resolution

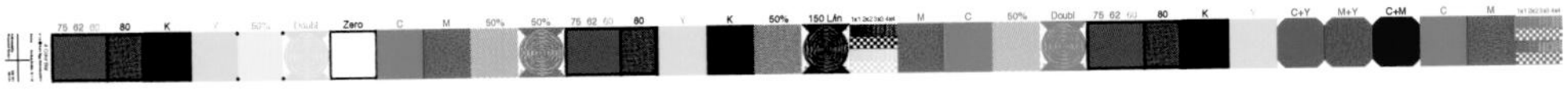

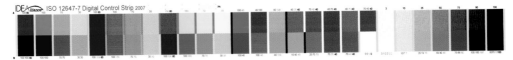

Figure 6.1.
An example of a color control bar. (Image courtesy of Franz Sigg.)

of the platesetter or the digital printing press. The layout of a color control bar requires that there be a white patch for measurement instrument calibration, a solid patch of each color repeated as often as possible (two ink keys in this case); and a single tint patch of each color repeated less frequently (every six ink keys in this case). Measurement across the width of the press sheet provides insights into inking uniformity. Measurement over time provides insights into inking consistency. Averages of solid coloration and TVI of CMYK channels provide a basis for assessing printing conformity. There is a registration mark at the beginning of the color control bar with text data, including the addressability (DPI) of the platesetter or PostScript version.

There is a three-color gray patch and a black tint patch every two ink keys. Dot areas of the gray patch (C75, M62, Y60) and the black tint (K80) should match each other colorimetrically and visually in a reference printing condition. These dot areas can be customized, for example, gray patch is (C50, M40, Y40) and the black tint is K50. The gray patch and the black tint can be measured and examined visually.

There is a dot-doubling patch in the form of concentric circles per color per repeat length. The concentric pattern is sensitive to directional dot gain at any angles. Thus, the dot-doubling patch helps to visually detect and explain why there is excessive dot gain in a pressrun. The checkerboard patterns, in the form of 1 × 1, 2 × 2, 3 × 3, and 4 × 4 clusters, for each color are used to monitor plate (CTP) exposure.

2. Color Proofing Bar

A color proofing bar, arranged in two tiers, is composed of a small number of color patches with known tonal values (Figure 6.2). In addition to single-color CMYK solids, CMYK midtone tints, and two-color RGB solids, a color proofing bar also contains single-color quarter-tone tints, three-quarter-tone tints, and neutral-neutral CMY tints. The color proofing bar is placed inside the contract color proof and is used for proofing assessment purposes.

Figure 6.2.
An example of a two-tier color proofing bar. (Image courtesy of Idealliance.)

3. Color Characterization Chart

A color characterization chart is composed of a large number of arrays of squares with known tonal values, including CMYK ramps. ISO 12642-2 (ISO, 2005a), as shown in Figure 3.6 (visual layout) and Figure 4.3 (random layout), specify 1617 CMYK patches. It is also known as the IT8.7/4 target. The chart is placed inside a press sheet or a color proof and is used for characterizing the printing/proofing conditions and constructing ICC profiles.

4. Resolution Target

A resolution target is an encapsulated PostScript (EPS) file, usually made from hand-coded PostScript codes, and is used to analyze the addressability and resolution of a digital imaging device. Figure 6.3 illustrates a resolution target made up of 5° wedges. The screen frequency increases as the wedge narrows to the center of the target. When reproduced by a high-resolution system, the target appears to be a uniform disk. When reproduced by a low-resolution system, the center of the target appears to be darker than the edge of the target.

Figure 6.3.
An example of a resolution target. (Image courtesy of Franz Sigg.)

6.3. Pictorial Test Elements

We use pictorial test elements in a test form to depict color image quality between various printing devices. Figure 6.4, "Bride and Groom," is one of the ISO 12640-3 SCID/CIELAB images (ISO, 2007a). SCID is the acronym for standard color image data.

CIELAB/SCID

Figure 6.4.
An example of an ISO 12640-3 SCID/ CIELAB image. (Reproduced with permission from ANSI on behalf of ISO. All rights reserved.)

Upon the B-to-A conversion and printing of the SCID images, we can examine the quality of the skin tone, the subtlety of the highlights in the wedding gown and the shadows in the tuxedo, the details of the bouquet, and the neutrality of the background, all in a single image. We can also visually assess color image quality of different printing conditions due to changes in substrate, gloss, solid ink density, and TVI.

Figure 6.5, 05_magenta, is one of the Roman16 bvdm pictorial reference images (bvdm, 2013). These test images are available in RGB color space and in CMYK color space. These pictorial images are used to assess similarities and differences of pictorial color image quality in different color reproduction conditions.

When correlating measured color difference and pictorial color image difference, it is possible to measure colors in an image as opposed to synthetic targets bearing no direct relation to the pictorial image. The Roman16 images, as shown in Figure 6.5, already include image-dependent pixels on either side of the pictorial image for this purpose.

6.4. Test Form Preparation

A test forms is a collection of test elements according to a signature layout. The test elements are often assembled in Adobe InDesign software according to the dimensions of the output device. Synthetic test elements in vector graphics are either hand-coded PostScript or from Adobe Illustrator software. Pictorial images are often prepared from Adobe Photoshop software. If the source images are in RGB or CIELAB color spaces, the color conversion should be explicit, for example, relative colorimetric rendering with black point compensation. The InDesign file is usually exported as a PDF/X file before sending it to the print server for proofing, platemaking, or digital printing.

Figure 6.6 is an example of a CMYK test form with dimensions of 26" × 20". Notice that a color control bar is placed at the top edge of the test form for solid coloration measurement and inking control. Two randomized color characterization (IT8.7/4) charts are included along with a P2P chart. ISO 12640-1 SCID/CMYK pictorial test images are also included to facilitate visual assessment (ISO, 1995).

There are additional features in the test form: (1) the background of the test form is near neutral (CMY), facilitating the ink consumption and printing-process control; and (2) a text box, explaining the purpose and the preparation of the test form. A sampling scheme may be included to identify sampled press sheets, whether the job is in its makeready, calibration, or production phase.

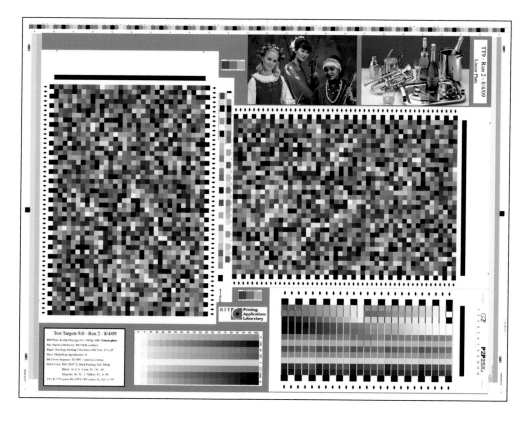

Figure 6.7 is a monochrome test form with dimensions of 8.5″ × 11″. The pictorial image comes from the ISO 12640-1 SCID/CMYK images. The gray scales, in steps and in vignette, are EPS files. The test form can be output to selected printers or proofers to study how engraving, solid ink density, TR, and TVI impact the appearance of the monochrome reproduction (Chung, 2006).

Figure 6.6.

An example of a CMYK test form. (Image courtesy of RIT Printing Applications Laboratory.)

Figure 6.7.

An example of a monochrome test form in letter-size.

6.5. Device Calibration

A test form is used to quantify color characteristics of an output device. If the initial results differ from the target values, there are two ways to introduce the adjustments: (1) physical and (2) digital data. Physical adjustments, for example, changes in press settings, changes in ink formulation, and changes in ink film thickness (IFT), should be made first. Digital data adjustments, that is, TVI and gray balance changes in prepress, should be done second.

Device calibration is the adjustment of a printing device, including physical adjustments and digital data adjustments, to conform to specified aim values. The basic premise is that color appearance of printed images among dissimilar devices can be aligned when the same calibration aims are used.

6.6. Process Control Metrics

A printing condition can be characterized by the relationship between CMYK (input) values and process control (output) metrics. Process control metrics are measurable factors that characterize some aspects of ink–paper–press conditions. Typical process control metrics used in press calibration and printing conformity assessment are presented below.

1. Solid Coloration

Solid coloration is paper and ink dependent. For example, coated (glossy) papers can print solids to higher C^* and lower L^* values than uncoated papers can; and high-chroma inks can achieve higher C^* than standard CMYK inks can. Solid coloration aims are specified as CIELAB values. Solid coloration tolerances are specified in ΔE^*_{ab} or ΔE_{00}.

A good question to ask is: Does higher ink film thickness (W) always produce higher solid ink density (D)? The answer is: No, solid ink densities (D) cannot be increased indefinitely. Saturation density (SD), per the Tollenaar equation (Tollenaar and Ernst, 1961), specifies the limit. As indicated in Eq. 6.1, D is the solid ink density of the print; SD is the density of an infinitely thick ink film; m is the rate at which SD is approached; and w is the relative ink film thickness.

$$D = SD(1 - e^{-mw})$$

Eq. 6.1

Figure 6.8 illustrates the nonlinear relationship between solid ink density (D) and ink film thickness of a print. In other words, solid ink density (D) cannot be increased indefinitely, and has to be tested.

Figure 6.8.

Saturation density (dotted line), as defined by the Tollenaar equation.

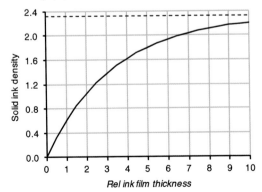

Printing-Process Control and Standardization

2. Color Gamut

Color gamut is 3-D and is expressed as a volume (cubic CIELAB units). It is convenient to express color gamut as a 2-D a^*b^* diagram (Figure 6.9). The larger the gamut, the more colorful the printed color. However, judging color matching using the a^*b^* diagram, without L^*, is deceiving. For example, primary colors and secondary overprints have the same a^* and b^* values, but we do not know whether these colors match, because L^* information is missing. In addition, we do not know whether in-gamut colors match, because we are missing TR and gray balance information.

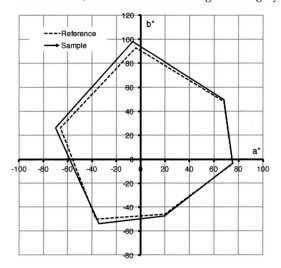

Figure 6.9.
2-D a^*b^* diagram of two CMYK printing conditions.

3. Tone Reproduction (TR) Curve and Tonal Value Increase (TVI) Curve

The TR and TVI curves are two sides of the same coin. The TR curve, as shown in Figure 6.10, is a graph comparing relative density of the print and % dot area. In this instance, the dotted line is a typical TR of AM (amplitude-modulated) 150 lines/inch screening, and the solid line is a typical TR of FM (frequency-modulated) 21 mm screening.

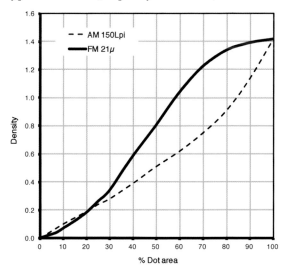

Figure 6.10.
TR curves.

The TVI curve, as shown in Figure 6.11, is a graph between TVI and % dot area. With the use of the Murray-Davies equation (chapter 1, Eq. 1.10), we can convert print density to tonal value (TV), and from TV to tonal value increase (TVI).

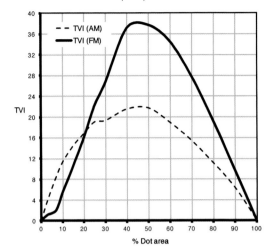

Figure 6.11.
TVI curves.

The solid line, having darker midtone density and more dot gain (TVI), is typical of FM printed reproduction. The dotted line is a typical AM printed reproduction. Both screenings have the same solid ink density (1.40), but different TVI values. TR curves are used to match TVIs of FM screening and AM screening (see section 6.8, "1-D Transfer Curves Method").

4. Midtone Spread (MTS)

MTS, as shown in chapter 1, Eq. 1.14, is a measure of TVI alignment among C, M, and Y channels. The formula appears more complicated than it is. As illustrated in Table 6.1, TVI values of the press sheet (labeled as x) are 12, 15, 18, and 20; and TVI aims (labeled as $x0$) are 16. We can calculate the difference as $(x - x0)$, identify the maximum of CMY and the minimum of CMY; the MTS is the difference between Max and Min. Notice that the black printer, K, is not involved in the MTS calculation.

Table 6.1. An example of an MTS calculation.

TVI	x	$x0$	$(x-x0)$	Max (CMY)	Min (CMY)	Max – Min
C	12	16	−4			
M	15	16	−1	+2	−4	+6
Y	18	16	+2			
K	20	16	+4			

5. Gray Balance (Near-Neutral) Triplets

Gray balance (near-neutral) triplets are TVs (Table 6.2) that appear achromatic when printed under specified printing and viewing conditions. CGATS TR 015 uses Equation 6.2 to define TVs of gray balance triplets, where magenta TV and yellow TV are a function of cyan TV (CGATS, 2013).

$$M = Y = 0.747C - 4.1\times10^{-4}C^2 + 2.94\times10^{-5}C^3 \qquad \text{Eq. 6.2}$$

Table 6.2. Tonal values of near-neutral triplets.

C	M	Y
0	0	0
10	7	7
20	15	15
25	19	19
30	23	23
40	31	31
50	40	40
60	50	50
70	60	60
75	66	66
80	72	72
90	85	85
100	100	100

6. Gray Reproduction

Gray reproduction refers to a set of colorimetric values (a^*, b^*) of the printed triplets that are achromatic. CGATS TR 015 defines gray reproduction aims as

$$a^*(\mathrm{TV_C}) = a^*_s \times \left(1 - \frac{\mathrm{TV_C}}{100}\right)$$ Eq. 6.3

$$b^*(\mathrm{TV_C}) = b^*_s \times \left(1 - \frac{\mathrm{TV_C}}{100}\right)$$ Eq. 6.4

where a^* ($\mathrm{TV_C}$) is modified a^*, b^* ($\mathrm{TV_C}$) is modified b^*, a^*_s is a^* of the substrate, b^*_s is b^* of the substrate, and $\mathrm{TV_C}$ is the cyan TV of the CMY triplets.

Figure 6.12 is an example of gray reproduction curves using linear plates in the initial pressrun. Equations 6.3 and 6.4 are used to construct the straight-line (dotted) gray reproduction from a^* and b^* values of the substrate and 0% TV.

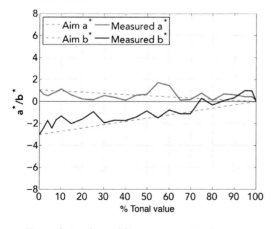

Figure 6.12.
Gray reproduction with a converging pattern.

To explain, the red line represents a^* measurements and the blue line represents b^* measurements of the gray balance triplets. The two lines show a converging pattern toward ($0a^*$, $0b^*$) as the cyan dot area goes to solid (100). In this case, the gray reproduction is in conformance using linear plates.

Figure 6.13 shows a nonconverging pattern of the gray reproduction in the initial pressrun (Chung and Wang, 2011b). For an arbitrary pressrun, the probability of resulting in a nonconverging (or fishtail) pattern is significantly higher than resulting in a converging gray reproduction at the CMY solids. This is because process ink pigments are not spectrally pure. In addition, we have little understanding of how ink trapping works at the CMY solids.

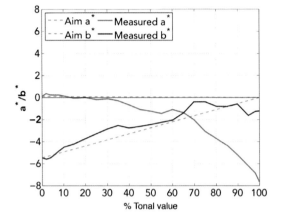

Figure 6.13.

Gray reproduction with a nonconverging (fishtail) pattern.

While nonconvergence at the CMY solids cannot be corrected by 1-D transfer curves, it does not negate the usefulness of controlling gray reproduction in printing-process control. This is because the CMY solids are not used in process color printing, that is, the shadow region of an image is limited by total area coverage (TAC) and gray component replacement (GCR) in color conversion. This is why larger gray reproduction tolerance is specified in three-quarter tone and the CMY solids in the G7 Pass/Fail Guidelines (Idealliance, 2018).

7. Chromaticness Difference (ΔC_h)

Chromaticness difference (ΔC_h), as shown in chapter 2, Eqs. 2.17–2.19, is the color difference between a measured gray balance triplet and its reference. In other words, ΔC_h uses the same formula as ΔE^*_{ab} by treating ΔL^* as "zero." The plot between chromaticness difference (ΔC_h) and TV is a measure of gray reproduction conformity.

6.7.   ISO/TS 10128: Device Calibration

Color image reproduction quality depends on color gamut. Color gamut depends on substrates (i.e., coated, uncoated, newsprint) and press physical settings (solid coloration, TVI, ink-down sequence, registration). Color image reproduction quality also depends on the adjustment of CMYK digital data (gray balance and tone reproduction).

CMYK digital data are device values, not color. The same CMYK file printed under different printing conditions (run 1) will produce different colors. When digital data are adjusted and printed (run 2) to reconcile the different printing conditions, device-to-device color agreement is achieved. In other words, press calibration takes two pressruns, that is, run 1 is used to find out where the press is, and run 2 is used to print the adjusted data to calibration aims.

ISO/TS 10128 describes three methods of digital data adjustment to achieve color agreement among presses calibrating to the same aim values (ISO, 2015a). These methods are (1) 1-D transfer curves, (2) predefined near neutrals, and (3) multidimensional transforms. Assumptions about each adjustment method and the procedure required are introduced first. Each is followed by a case study.

6.8. 1-D Transfer Curves Method

6.8.1. Assumptions

Once the correct process color solids and two-color overprint solids are achieved in the initial pressrun (run 1), a press can be calibrated by matching the measured TV curve to the specified TV curve for each primary (run 2). In other words, the initial pressrun (run 1) requires material selections and physical adjustments on press to achieve solid coloration; and the calibration pressrun (run 2) requires the adjustment of input (digital) values to align TVI values. The 1-D transfer curves method is also known as the "dot gain compensation" method.

6.8.2. Procedure to Generate a 1-D Transfer Curves

a. Conduct run 1 by using plates made from known platemaking conditions and printing to the required solid coloration.

   When the press sheet is printed by an offset lithographic press, the ink film is wet initially. Wet ink densities are higher than dry ink densities. The phenomenon is known as density dry-back. Because the aim densities are based on dry ink measurement, the loss of density due to ink dry-back must be addressed by aiming at higher wet densities. Alternatively, apply an aqueous coating or use UV curing inks to alleviate the concern for ink dry-back.

b. Enter two TR curves, that is, a reference and a sample (run 1), for each process color channel.

c. Find the 1-D transfer curve by identifying %TV pairs that yield the same relative density between the two TR curves.

d. Send the transfer curves to a RIP (raster image processor) to alter the device values for each channel to produce the curved plates.

e. Use the curved plates to conduct run 2 by repeating run 1 printing conditions.

6.9. Case Study: Matching AM and FM Tone Reproduction

Screening is the process of converting digital data (pixels, bits, bytes) into halftone dots. Amplitude-modulated (AM) screening is the default screening whereby halftone dots vary in sizes, but with equal frequency (lines per inch). Frequency-modulated (FM) screening renders digital data into micro dots of equal size, but with varying frequency.

Figure 6.14 illustrates two photomicrographs of the eye from the ISO 12640-1 SCID/CMYK pictorial test image, "Three Musicians," printed from run 1 with linear plates. The left-hand-side eye, rendered by FM screening, appears to be darker with more image details than the right-hand-side eye, rendered by AM screening.

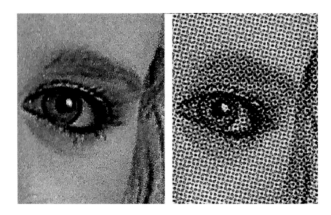

Figure 6.14.
Photomicrograph of FM (left) and AM (right) screening before tonal adjustments.

The method of matching AM and FM tone reproduction by the "1-D Transfer Curves," as specified in ISO/TS 10128, was called the "dot gain compensation" method (Chung and Ma, 1995).

As shown in Figure 6.15 (left), FM screening (solid line) has higher TVI than AM screening (dotted line), thus, appearing darker. Figure 6.15 (left) also illustrates the use of a 1-D transfer curve to reconcile the TR difference between AM and FM screening. In this instance, the TR curves have the same relative solid ink density (1.40). The 150 lpi AM screening is the dotted line, and the FM screening is the solid line. "Matching AM and FM TR" means using the two TR curves to find %TV pairs that yield equal relative density between 0 and 100 TV. We can use the ray-tracing technique to find %TV pairs, as shown below:

a. Identify a TV, for example, 50%.

b. Locate the density value (0.51) from the AM screening.

c. Trace the TVs of the FM screening (37%) that also produces the same density (0.51).

d. Construct the 1-D transfer curve, as shown in Figure 6.15 (right), based on the %TV pairs (50%, 37%), and

e. Repeat the above steps for other tonal vales and process colors.

Figure 6.15
Ray-tracing to find 1-D adjustment curve.

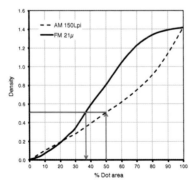
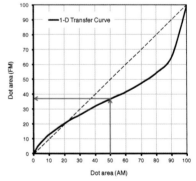

6.10. Predefined Near-Neutrals Method

The "predefined near-neutrals" method, defined in CGATS TR 015, specifies TR and gray balance aims based on predefined 3-C neutrals for any CMYK printing process (CGATS, 2013). The use of predefined 3-C neutrals, specified in chapter 6, Eq. 6.2, recognizes that a^* and b^* values of the paper substrate are the beginning of the gray balance. This means that when a^* and b^* values of the substrate are not 0, the eye will adapt and see the substrate as neutral, a phenomenon called chromatic adaptation (see also chapter 2, section 2.24). Equations 6.3 and 6.4 are used to provide a linear transition for a^* and b^* values of the predefined 3-C neutrals between the color of the substrate and the target color of the 3-C solid.

Before the introduction of the predefined near-neutrals method, two RIT researchers devised a method of finding the desired color separation for correct gray balance and TR in specified ink–paper–press conditions (Elyjiw and Archer, 1972). This method finds CMY dot area combinations that would produce neutrals for an ink–paper–press condition, as opposed to adjusting a CMYK file to a set of predefined CMY dot areas and printing them as neutrals.

6.10.1. Assumption

The predefined near-neutrals method is based on the idea that gray balance and tone reproduction can be addressed as a part of the press calibration, such that pictorial color images, when reproduced in different ink–paper–press conditions, share common color appearance without the ICC color-management system.

While TVI accounts for printing variations of single inks, printed colors are also impacted by the interaction of two-color and three-color overprints. Hence, TV adjustment curves, based on gray reproduction aims, should provide better color appearance matches among devices than the 1-D transfer curves method. The predefined near-neutrals method is also known as the G7 method (Idealliance, 2014).

6.10.2. Procedure to Generate and Assess Curved Plates based on Predefined Near Neutrals

CGATS TR 015 specifies what a predefined near-neutral scale is and its tone reproduction characteristics. Idealliance published the G7 methodology and offers G7 training programs with a focus on how to calibrate any ink–paper–press condition, including using customized software packages, like Curve3, Curve4, SpotOn, etc.

Assuming that the press was calibrated and press sheets sampled, the following procedure can be used to assess conformance to predefined near neutrals.

a. Verify tone values of predetermined near-neutral triplets (Eq. 6.2).

b. Measure the production paper color.

c. Calculate gray reproduction aims (a^*, b^*) of the triplets, using Eqs. 6.3 and 6.4.

d. Measure CIELAB values of printed triplets.

e. Assess the chromaticness difference (ΔC_h) of near-neutral triplets and $a*$ and $b*$ versus %dot of the job.

6.11. Case Study: G7 Press Calibration

This case study describes the G7 calibration using the Presstek 52DI waterless sheetfed offset press, FM screening, Toyo waterless inks, and Endurance coated paper at RIT.

Figure 6.16 is the P2P51 (input) target, including the predefined near-neutral triplets (column 4) and a K-only ramp (column 5). Color measurements are carried out using a X-Rite i1 Pro2 spectro-densitometer.

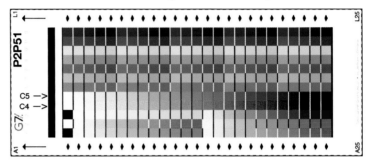

Figure 6.16.
P2P51 target.
(Image courtesy of
Idealliance.)

The initial pressrun 1 was carried out using linear plates. The printing aim was GRACoL 2006. The measurement data were analyzed using Curve3 software to assess solid coloration, tone reproduction, and gray reproduction. Figure 6.17 illustrates the solid coloration conformity. Both solid ink densities and CIELAB values of single-color CMYK solids and two-color (RGB) overprints are shown, along with the color difference (ΔE_{00}) in relation to solid printing aims.

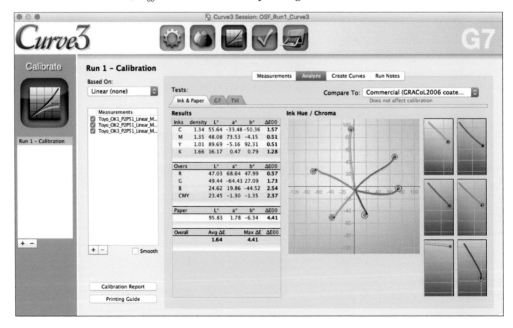

Figure 6.17.
Assessment of solid
coloration (run 1).

Figure 6.18 illustrates tone reproduction and gray balance of the initial (run 1) printing condition. In this instance, the TR (displayed in red) is not in conformity, but the gray balance (displayed in green) is in conformity. Notice that $\Delta L^* = L^*(\text{Sample}) - L^*(\text{Reference})$. When ΔL^* is negative, the sample is too dark, and the corrective action is to reduce TVs in the midtone. Also notice that when the gray balance is in conformity, the ΔC_h (green line) plot has small deviation throughout the TVs.

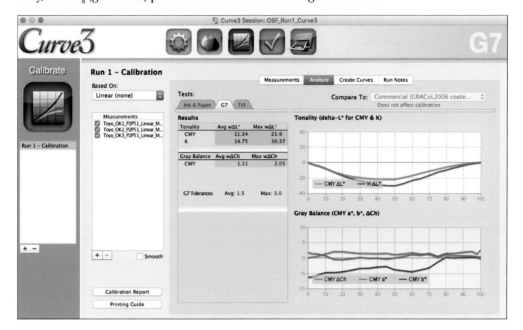

Figure 6.19 illustrates the use of Curve3 software to derive the adjustment curves for each color channel. In this example, FM TVs of all four CMYK channels are reduced to match the tonality of the GRACoL 2006 aims.

Figure 6.18.
Assessment of TR and gray balance (run 1).

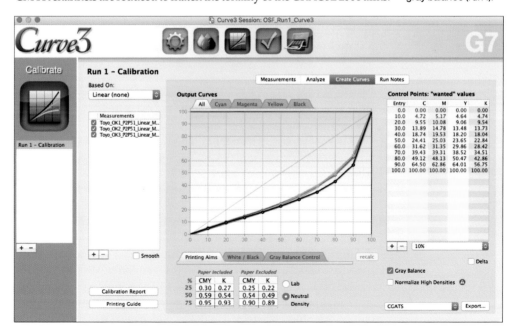

The adjustment curves are used to alter the device values for each channel during the CTP operation. Upon printing (run 2), we can reassess tone reproduction and gray balance of the adjusted printing conditions.

Figure 6.19.
Deriving 1-D adjustment curves.

Figure 6.20 illustrates that the tone reproduction and gray reproduction are in conformity using the predefined near-neutrals calibration method.

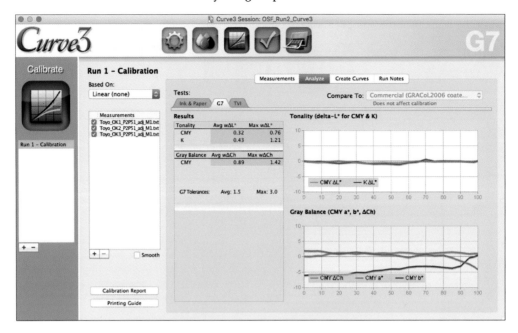

Figure 6.20.
Assessment of the calibrated printing condition (run 2).

6.12. Multidimensional Transforms Method

6.12.1. Assumption

Multidimensional transforms use complex computations to process color data between the reference printing condition and the sample printing or proofing condition. In addition, color and transparency of the primaries between the sample printing condition and the reference printing condition do not have to be the same. The multidimensional transforms method is also known as the device-link method.

6.12.2. Procedure

a. Start from job data in reference or source CMYK color space.
b. Build a device-link profile by identifying the source color space, the destination color space, and the rendering intent.
c. Use the device-link API (application programming interface) to convert CMYK data from the reference CMYK color space into the destination CMYK color space.
d. Output the converted data in the destination color space.

6.13. Case Study: Color Proofing using the Device-Link Method

A device-link profile is a type of ICC profile that is used to modify the standard CMYK data, to enable the results proofed on a specific proofing device to match the appearance of the standard CMYK data as if it has been printed on the standard press. Chapter 9, section 9.10, "SCCA Case Study 2: Proof and Print to Substrate-corrected Colorimetric Aims," reports a case study whereby (1) a device-link profile was used to match the substrate-corrected (M1) data set when printing with a Goss Sunday 2000 web offset press and Sappi Opus paper (containing optical brightening agents), and (2) another device-link profile was used to match the same SCCA data set using a proofer and the standard proofing substrate.

Alwan LinkProfiler was used to construct the device-link profiles. The results show that proofing and printing to the same substrate-corrected data set (M1) provide proof–print color match better than the near-neutral calibration method.

6.14. Chapter Summary

CMYK data are device values, not colors. The same CMYK file printed under different printing conditions will produce different colors and thus will look different. Modification of the digital data can be used to adjust differences in press, ink, and paper between the actual conditions and the standard printing condition.

ISO/TS 10128 specifies three press-calibration methods to align dissimilar printing conditions. Two methods use 1-D adjustment curves and assume similar color and transparency of the inks between the reference printing condition and the sample (or actual) printing condition. They are easy to implement and are applicable to CTP and conventional printing.

The above assumptions are not required when ICC device-link profiles are used to implement CMYK-to-CMYK transforms between the source printing condition and the destination printing condition. ICC device-link profiles are applicable to color proofing and digital printing.

Calibration works only in stable or repeatable printing conditions. All three calibration methods discussed in this chapter assume printing repeatability. We can determine the repeatability of a printing device by measuring and analyzing printed color bars over time. When the printing device is found to be unstable or outside tolerance limits, calibration should be aborted and the ink–paper–press conditions investigated and corrected until they are brought back to a stable printing condition.

6.15. Multiple-Choice and Essay Questions

1. ISO/TS 10128 specifies _____ methods for adjusting within-gamut data to match a set of characterization data.
   A. two
   B. three
   C. four
   D. five

2. The _____ aims are straight lines beginning from a^* and b^* values of the substrate.
   A. tone reproduction (TR)
   B. gray reproduction
   C. solid ink density
   D. color gamut

3. The gray reproduction metric specifies _____ of the printed near-neutral triplets.
   A. L^*
   B. a^*
   C. b^*
   D. a^* and b^*

4. Midtone spread (MTS) is derived from _____.
A. TVIs of CMY
B. TVIs of CMYK
C. CIELAB values of a C50 M40Y40 patch
D. None of the above

5. _____ is a good solution for reconciling amplitude-modulated (AM) and frequency-modulated (FM) screening differences.
A. Matching tonal value (TV) curves
B. Using predefined near neutrals
C. Using the multidimensional transforms
D. The trial and error method

6. The G7 calibration method requires the use of _____.
A. tonal value (TV) curves
B. predefined near neutrals
C. multidimensional transforms
D. the trial and error approach

7. _____ accomplish press calibration by means of a device-link profile.
A. Multidimensional transforms
B. Predefined near neutrals
C. Four 1-D adjustment curves
D. All of the above

8. Synthetic test elements are used to find out the _____ of a printing device.
A. resolution
B. tonality
C. color characteristics
D. All of the above

9. Without press calibration, the same CMYK file will produce _____ under different printing conditions.
A. identical colors
B. pleasing colors
C. different colors
D. perfect color matches

10. ISO/TS 10128 is based on the modification of _____ to adjust differences in press, ink and paper.
A. digital data
B. press speed
C. paper gloss
D. screening

11. Define the term *device calibration* in process color printing. How is it accomplished?

12. What is the relationship between ink film thickness and solid ink density, according to the Tollenaar equation?

7 Printing-Process Control

Printing-process control involves knowing printing aims, how to sample, what to measure, required analyses, and what to adjust in prepress and printing in order to achieve conformity. After reading this chapter, one should become aware that printing conformity and printing-process control are intertwined in relation to analog printing and digital printing.

7.1. Terminology

The term *accuracy* is a measure of deviation between the sample average and the aim point. Deviation, attributed to assignable causes, can be reconciled through calibration, that is, adjustments in prepress or printing to match the aim points.

The term *precision* is a measure of variation or closeness among sample measurements and the average of these measurements or production center. Aim points are not involved in the estimation of precision.

The term *specifications* represents product requirements, including aim points and tolerances.

The term *process capability* represents what a production can do, including production deviation and production variation.

7.2. Three Aspects of Product Specifications

From a statistical process control (SPC) point of view, there are three aspects of product specifications: (1) calibration deviation using initial samples and the aim point; (2) production deviation using multiple samples in subsequent production (production center) and the aim; and (3) production variation using multiple samples in subsequent production and the production center.

Figure 7.1 is a schematic of calibration deviation, that is, the color difference between initial sheets (2-3) and the aim point, indicated by the red line. For simplicity's sake, tolerance for calibration deviation is shown as a circle in Δa^* and Δb^* coordinates.

Figure 7.2 is a schematic of production deviation and production variation. Production deviation is the color difference between production center and the aim, indicated by the red line. If the production deviation of the first job is 4 ΔE and the production deviation of the second

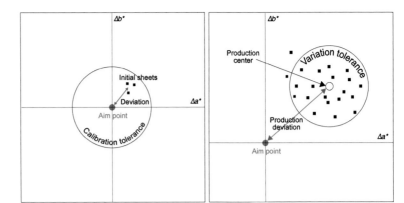

Left: **Figure 7.1.**
Calibration deviation.

Right: **Figure 7.2.**
Production deviation and production variation.

job is 4 Δ*E*, what is the color difference between the two print jobs? The answer is: We don't know. This is because Δ*E* is only a magnitude. Unless we know the color coordinates of the two production centers, the color difference between the two jobs, or job-to-job color variation, can be anywhere from 0 to 8 Δ*E*.

Production variation is the color difference between production center and individual sample measurements. It is also called within-job color variation. In Figure 7.2, tolerance for production variation is shown as a circle in Δ*a** and Δ*b** coordinates.

It would have been ideal if sampling and test methods for printing conformity and printing-process control were dovetailed. But, this is not the case due to different timing and standards development paths. A case in point is that Dolezalek (1994) studied production variation of 19 pressruns by colorimetry before the development of ISO 12647-2. He defined production deviation as the color difference between the production center and the OK sheet (not the aim). Dolezalek's work had profound influence on the development of the ISO 12647 series of printing standards from 1990s to the present day. The misalignment between product conformity and printing-process control remains. See section 9.15, "Future Revision of ISO 12647-2: Offset Lithographic Processes," for further discussion.

7.3. Printing-Process Control

Process control should be based on process capability and control limits, and not based on tolerances. In this book, printing-process control is modeled by three steps, shown in Figure 7.3. The first (makeready) step is to set printing aims, control limits, and initial ink film thickness (IFT). The second (calibration) step addresses inking adjustments, based on sampling and measurement, to achieve calibration conformity. The third (process control) step continues the sample–measure–adjust cycle to achieve production conformity in the subsequent production.

Figure 7.3.
A generic printing-process control flowchart.

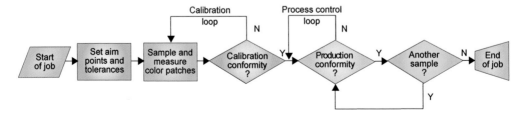

The strategy in printing-process control is to (1) identify factors that impact color accuracy and color consistency, (2) know what to measure, what to control, and when to control, and (3) leave random variation (noise) alone.

Factors that impact printing-process control include (1) selecting printing aims; (2) sampling press sheets; (3) measuring, inspecting, and decision-making; (4) adjusting solid coloration using Beer's law; and (5) adjusting gray balance. These factors are discussed next.

7.4. Selecting Printing Aims

Analog printing technology, that is, printing with plates or cylinders, includes offset, flexographic, and gravure printing. Printing-process control begins with selecting printing aims and is followed by press calibration. In terms of material control, process inks are standardized and paper stocks are categorized. In terms of prepress adjustments, printing-image carriers (plates and cylinders) are made with the use of tonal transfer curves to achieve either TVI conformity or gray balance conformity. In terms of process control, ink film thickness or solid ink density are adjusted to achieve solid coloration or gray balance conformity.

ISO 12647-2 has been widely adapted as the printing aims in high-volume analog printing markets, including publication, newspaper, and commercial printing (2013a). It specifies ISO 2846-1 (2006) compliant process color inks. For specified paper grades, the standard also specifies process control metrics, that is, solid coloration and TVI, as printing aims.

Digital printing technology, that is, printing without plates or masters, includes electrophotography and inkjet printing. Toners and inkjet colorants are not standardized. Process control is primarily via software adjustments. In this case, tonal transfer curves and device-link profiles are used to simulate a specified reference printing condition or customized characterization data set.

ISO/PAS 15339-1 has been adapted recently as the printing aims in digital printing markets (2015c). It specifies the color characterization data set as press calibration aims. This standard does not specify process control metrics (i.e., TVI, predefined near neutrals, or device-link profile). This standard requires a dedicated test form (e.g., chapter 6, Figure 6.6) to assess the calibration conformity.

7.5. Sampling Press Sheets

Press sheets, containing job data, vary from pressrun to pressrun. To enable printing-process control, press sheets should contain a color control bar with specific color patches of known values, situated in the trim of the press sheet.

While we can never be certain that we have complete randomization, we can look for signs of non-randomness by observing data collected in sequence. Figure 7.4 illustrates two scenarios of sampling, that is, if only C1, C2, C3, and C4 are sampled and measured, it tells a different story if more data, including those data points in red, were sampled.

Press sheet sampling plays an important role in how we interpret production deviation and production variation. Although samples are collected sequentially as print production progresses, it is important that a sample is picked randomly without any inspection. For all practical purposes, two or three samples are recommended for calibration

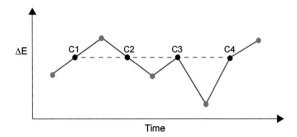

Figure 7.4.
Two scenarios of sampling.

conformity assessment, and 15–20 samples are recommended for production conformity assessment.

7.6. Measuring, Inspecting, and Decision-making

In a sheetfed offset printing environment, press sheets are measured in order to control the print production. Press sheets are also examined visually. Some questions to ask: "Can I correlate between instrumental color difference and visual color difference?," "Can I tell if the process is within its normal variation?," "If the process requires corrective action, do I know what to control and by how much?"

When printing was a craft, visual inspection was key in detecting color differences between the color proof (or OK sheet) and sample press sheets. By laying sample press sheets with the color bars exposed (Figure 7.5), the technique of *press sheet shingling* allows press operators to visually examine inking uniformity across the sheet and to assess color consistency from sheet to sheet.

Figure 7.5.
Press sheet shingling.

The downside of inspecting and controlling color visually is that (1) it is difficult to document the eyeball-based control; (2) it is easy to tamper with the process, that is, making unnecessary or wrong adjustments; (3) high waste and spoilage are probable; and (d) printing quality is operator-dependent (Chung, 1991).

As printing became a manufacturing process, color-measurement and statistical process control (SPC) software became the basis for process control. Color-measurement tools are used to detect color differences between printed samples and color aims. SPC software turns data into information and provides tangible evidence for process adjustments. SPC tools also eliminate guesswork. The downside of controlling color by SPC is that (1) there are substantial hardware and software investments, and (2) there is a learning curve in using SPC tools effectively on press.

Decision making should be data driven. But do not make a decision based on one sample alone. This is because when there is only one datum, we know nothing about the variation of the process. It is recommended that 2–3 initial press sheets be sampled for calibration deviation assessment and 20 press sheets be sampled for production deviation and production variation assessment.

Making frequent changes can lead to tampering with the process. Let's use a pressman's narrative to understand the relationship between press sheet sampling, press speed, and inking adjustment. Let's give the pressman a name, so it's easier to follow. The pressman's name is Joe.

Joe runs a sheetfed offset press typically at 12,000 impressions per hour (iph). This is equivalent to 200 impressions per minute (ipm). When Joe makes a moderate inking change on the press, it takes 300 impressions to realize the effect. Thus, the sampling interval should be 1.5 minutes, or 90 seconds. When Joe's sampling interval is shorter than 90 seconds and he makes frequent inking adjustments, he may face the consequence of making adjustments based on changing printing conditions.

7.7. Adjusting Solid Coloration using Beer's Law

In printing-process control, a key variable that can be adjusted during printing is ink film thickness (IFT). There are two competing approaches in IFT control in process color printing: (a) adjusting IFT to minimize solid coloration variation, that is, keeping the outer-gamut color consistent; and (b) adjusting IFT to minimize tone reproduction and gray balance variation, that is, keeping in-gamut color consistent.

According to ISO/TS 10128 (2015a), the first step in device calibration is to adjust IFT to meet solid coloration requirements. The second step is to adjust digital values to achieve TVI or gray balance conformity. In other words, adjusting ink film thickness to maintain solid coloration is common in realizing both TVI and gray balance conformity.

"Adjusting solid coloration" means adjusting the ink film thickness of CMYK solids to minimize color difference or density difference during the pressrun. Figure 7.6 is a flowchart for regulating solid coloration during a pressrun. It assumes that the printing conditions, including solid coloration aims and control limits, are known. Operationally, the first (calibration) loop is to adjust IFT of CMYK based on solid ink density; and to verify that solid coloration is in conformity in terms of CIELAB and ΔE^*_{ab}. The second (process control) loop continues the sample–measure–adjust cycle until the end of the job.

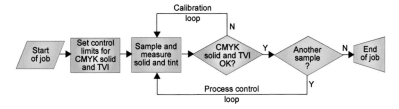

Figure 7.6. A SID-based printing-process control flowchart.

Beer's law provides a mathematical model regarding changes in solid ink density that best matches the specified CIELAB values. Beer's law (or the Beer-Lambert law) states that there is a linear relationship between concentration of the *material* and *attenuation of light*. In printing, the *material* is ink film thickness, and the *attenuation of light* is spectral reflectance of the ink. As shown in Eq. 7.1, Beer's law assumes that the ink film thickness is far from reaching its saturation density (Tollenaar and Ernst, 1961).

$$R_\lambda = 10^{-\{[(D_\lambda - D_p) \cdot t] + D_p\}}$$

Eq. 7.1

R_λ is spectral reflectance of the simulated sample, D_λ is spectral density of the measured sample, D_p is spectral density of the paper, and t is the ink film thickness ratio. There is no change when $t = 1.0$. When $t > 1.0$, density increases and reflectance decreases; when $t < 1.0$, density decreases and reflectance increases.

To adopt Beer's law in printing, the spectral absorption of the paper must be subtracted out, $(D_\lambda - D_p)$, to model ink film thickness changes. Later, the spectral absorption of the paper is added back in, $[(D_\lambda - D_p) \cdot t] + D_p$, to model the spectral reflectance of the ink at a given wavelength. Below are steps to put Eq. 7.1 into action:

1. Enter reference CIELAB values of CMYK solids.

2. Enter measured spectral data of paper and CMYK solids and compute their density and CIELAB values.

3. Use Beer's law to simulate spectral reflectance at different ink film thicknesses, that is, t ranging from 0.5 to 1.5 at 0.1 increments.

4. Use tristimulus integration, covered in section 2.9, to compute CIELAB and density values of simulated ink film thicknesses.

5. Generate a solid ink density (SID) versus ΔE_{00} graph for each of the CMYK inks (Figure 7.7).

6. Report the SID that produces the lowest ΔE_{00} for each ink.

Figure 7.7 is an example illustrating the prediction based on a measured spectral reflectance of a cyan solid and paper that includes (1) density and CIELAB values of the measured cyan sample, (2) ΔE_{00} between the measured cyan sample and the reference, and (3) required SID change and the best match in terms of ΔE_{00}.

Beer's law is also expressed in terms of spectral reflectance, as shown in Eq. 7.2. The derivation from Eq. 7.2 to Eq. 7.1 is documented in Appendix B.

$$R_\lambda = R_p \cdot \left[\frac{R_s}{R_p}\right]^t$$

Eq. 7.2

In summary, Beer's law, based on the color measurement of the initial press sheets, enables (1) the calculation of CIELAB values as a function of density of simulated press sheets at different ink film thicknesses, and (2) the ΔE_{00} prediction between the predicted CIELAB values and the printing aims. Many commercially available process control software packages offer spectrophotometer interfaces as well as graphical user interfaces for solid coloration adjustment on press.

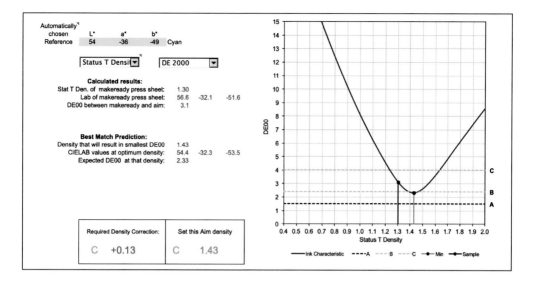

Automatically chosen
Reference | L* | a* | b*
| 54 | -36 | -49 | Cyan

Status T Density | DE 2000

Calculated results:
Stat T Den. of makeready press sheet: 1.30
Lab of makeready press sheet: 56.6 -32.1 -51.6
DE00 between makeready and aim: 3.1

Best Match Prediction:
Density that will result in smallest DE00: 1.43
CIELAB values at optimum density: 54.4 -32.3 -53.5
Expected DE00 at that density: 2.33

Required Density Correction:	Set this Aim density
C +0.13	C 1.43

Status T Density

— Ink Characteristic   ---- A   --- B   --- C   —●— Min   —●— Sample

7.8. Adjusting Gray Balance

Adjusting gray balance means adjusting the three-color (CMY) solids to minimize ΔL^* and ΔC_h of predefined triplets during the pressrun. Figure 7.8 illustrates a gray-based ink film thickness adjustment flowchart that provides clues as to which ink to change or whether to increase or decrease the ink films, but without the specific magnitude of change.

Figure 7.7.
Predicting solid ink density by Beer's law.

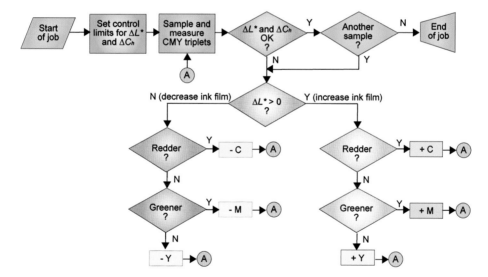

Figure 7.8.
A gray-based printing-process control flowchart.

The flowchart, in an abbreviated form, encompasses both the calibration loop and the process control loop. To explain,

1. Set aim points and control limits for gray balance metrics, ΔL^* and ΔC_h.

2. For calibration control, sample and measure a press sheet containing near-neutral CMY patches and solid ink patches.

3. Compute ΔL^*, chromaticness difference (ΔC_h), and Δh between the sample and the aims (sample – aim).

4. If either ΔC_h or ΔL^* exceeds the control limits, then

    a. If $\Delta L^* > 0$ (sample is too light) and
- Hue is too red, increase the cyan IFT (+C); return to Sample and measure via connector A.
- Hue is too green, increase the magenta IFT (+M); return to Sample and measure via connector A.
- Hue is too blue, increase the yellow IFT (+Y); return to Sample and measure via connector A.

    b. If $\Delta L^* < 0$ (sample is too dark) and
- Hue is too red, decrease the cyan IFT (–C); return to Sample and measure via connector A.
- Hue is too green, decrease the magenta IFT (–M); return to Sample and measure via connector A.
- Hue is too blue, decrease the yellow IFT (–Y); return to Sample and measure via connector A.

    c. Else, it signifies the calibration conformity.

5. For printing-process control, continue the sampling and repeat the Sample–Measure–Compare cycle via connector A, in the subsequent production until the end of the pressrun.

Figure 7.9 illustrates a two-tier color control bar. The top tier consists of an interlocking pattern of C50M40Y40 gray tints and K-only tints; the bottom tier consists of CMYK solids, CMYK 50% tints, and one C50M40Y40 gray tint. A color-measurement station, standard viewing booth, and visual inspection are required for the implementation.

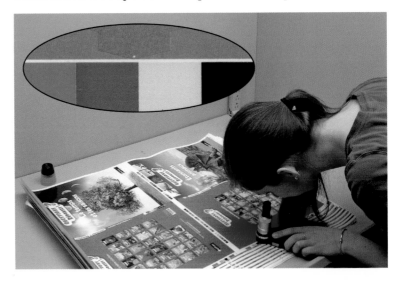

Figure 7.9.
A two-tier color bar for visual and quantitative assessment. (Image courtesy of D-Tone.)

To use the two-tier color bar in offset printing, (1) specify printing (gray) aims; (2) sample press sheets and scan the color bar; (3) adjust ink film thickness and ink–water balance until solids and TVIs are in conformity; (4) verify that the gray bar is uniform, that is, the interlocking pattern is not visible, side to side; (5) use the gray-based IFT adjustment algorithm for printing-process control (Figure 7.8); and (6) monitor visual consistency of the gray tints during the pressrun for added assurance.

Controlling gray balance during printing is more complicated than controlling solid coloration, because there is no "gray-balance knob" on a printing press. In addition to solid ink film thickness, there are other independent variables, (e.g., image content, gray component replacement [GCR], and dot slur/doubling) that also impact gray balance during printing. These variables are discussed next.

7.9. Effect of Image Content on Gray Balance

First, let's discuss the effect of image content on gray balance. Pictorial color images are characterized by tone (light, dark), color (hue, chroma), contrast (sharp, blur), and resolution (high, low). When reproducing pictorial color images using process color inks (CMYK), image content can influence gray balance of printed pictorial color images.

Felix Brunner (1987) pioneered the research that addressed the question, "Does the visual impact of gray balance variation depend on the content of color image?" The following procedures are used to simulate the visual impact of TVI variation of color images using Adobe Photoshop.

1. Open two pictorial color (RGB) images with different image characteristics, for example, a colorful image with multi-hue and an image with important neutrals and limited hues.

2. Select a near-neutral area in the image to remove color cast by using the gray balance Eyedropper.

3. Convert the RGB image to a three-channel CMY (No_K) image.

4. Alter TVI channel by channel in Photoshop. Figure 7.10 shows four TVI alterations with the straight-line or no black change (upper left); +4% cyan TVI change (upper right); +4% magenta TVI change (lower right); and +4% yellow TVI change (lower left).

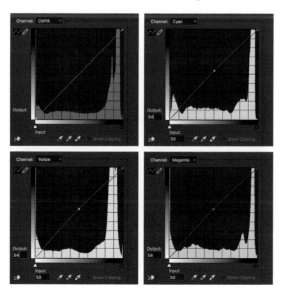

Figure 7.10.
Channel-by-channel TVI alteration.

5. Simulate printing variations of a gray patch by using the Eyedropper to sample a neutral area of the image, and fill the entire image with the gray value.

6. Convert all the CMY images and CMY gray patches as Lab files and assemble them in PowerPoint (Figures 7.11–7.13).

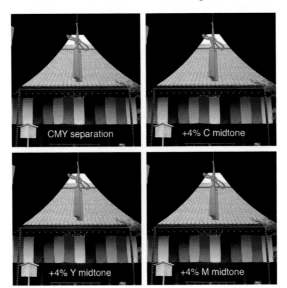

Figure 7.11.
Simulation of printing variation of a colorful image. (Image courtesy of Jim Shyu.)

Figure 7.11, "A Temple in Kyoto," is an image characterized by colorful banners. The upper left image is the CMY separation without TVI alteration, the upper right image is the +4% cyan alteration, the lower right image is the +4% magenta alteration, and the lower left image is the +4% yellow alteration.

Figure 7.12, "A Camel Ride in Inland China," is an image of a large area of near neutral with limited hues. The same procedures were used to prepare the TVI variations.

Figure 7.12.
Simulation of printing variation of a near-neutral image.

Figure 7.13 illustrates four gray patches. They are sampled, per Step 5 of the procedures, using the Eyedropper to sample a neutral area of the "A Camel Ride in Inland China" image (identified as a white square), and fill the entire image with the gray value.

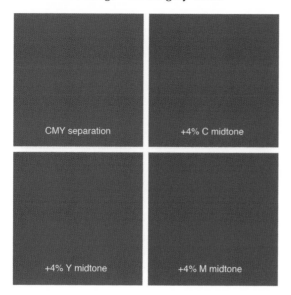

Figure 7.13.
Simulation of printing variation of a CMY-gray patch.

The three illustrations all have the same TVI alterations. But their visual impacts on gray balance are different from image to image. We can see that (1) the eye is less sensitive to pictorial images containing colorful multi-hues, (2) the eye is more sensitive to pictorial images containing large near neutrals with limited hues, and (3) the eye is most sensitive to a CMY-gray patch. In other words, the visual impact of TVI variation depends on image content. This is why monitoring a CMY-gray patch in conjunction with a matching black tint is strategic in four-color printing-process control.

7.10. Effect of GCR on Gray Balance

Second, let's examine the effect of GCR on gray balance. Gray component replacement (GCR) is the process of removing some chromatic process inks and replacing them with the equivalent black ink. The GCR amount is a color separation setting during the ICC profile creation process. GCR is also an ink optimization strategy. The performance of GCR depends on printing consistency.

Recognizing that a color can be built through different CMYK combinations, we can use the following example and procedures in Adobe Photoshop to demonstrate the effect of GCR on gray balance during printing.

1. Launch Adobe Photoshop and verify that the CMYK working space is GRACoL2013_CRPC6.

2. Enter the CIELAB values ($31L^*$, $7a^*$, and $2b^*$) in the Color Picker. In doing so, the B-to-A look-up table of the CMYK profile is used, and the CMYK builds (C25, M38, Y24, and K66) and a brownish color are displayed (Figure 7.14) The GCR setting of the GRACoL2013_CRPC6 ICC profile is considered medium to high.

Figure 7.14.
B-to-A color conversion using the Color Picker in Photoshop.

3. By entering 0 for the black channel and 80 for the other (CMY) channels, as shown in Figure 7.15, the A-to-B look-up table of the GRACoL2013_CRPC6 ICC profile is used, and the resulting CIELAB values (31L^*, 7a^*, and 2b^*) are the same as before, but with a very different CMYK build (C80, M80, Y80, K0).

Figure 7.15.
A-to-B color conversion using the Color Picker in Photoshop.

Thus, the same color can be printed using different CMYK combinations, also known as *CMYK build*. As shown in Figure 7.16, two different GCR settings can produce the same color when the printing process is accurate and consistent. When printing variation occurs, the low-GCR color image is subject to larger color variation than the high-GCR color image.

Figure 7.16.
Two different GCR settings that produce the same color.

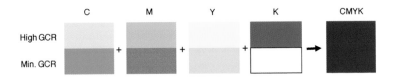

Printing-Process Control and Standardization

For high-volume printing, high GCR is used not only to minimize visual impact of color shift during printing, but also for ink cost savings, because the black ink costs less than chromatic inks. But the success of high-GCR color reproduction depends on the stability of the black printer. If there is excessive variation of the black printer, reduced image contrast can result.

7.11. Effect of Dot Slur/Doubling on Gray Balance

Dot slur/doubling darkens midtone, intermittently and directionally, and is caused by wavy papers, web tensions, and ink back-trap in offset printing. Independent of solid coloration, dot slur/doubling influences TVI and gray balance of color image reproduction.

Dot slur/doubling can be observed visually from the printed dot slur/doubling target (Figure 7.17). In the absence of dot slur/doubling, the two parallel patches (H and V) match each other. When dot slur/doubling occurs, the parallel line patch (H), perpendicular to the printing direction, is visually darker than the other parallel line patch (V). Dot slur/doubling can also be quantified using Eq. 1.9 in chapter 1, "Densitometry."

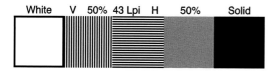

Figure 7.17.
Dot slur/doubling target.
(Image courtesy of Franz Sigg.)

Test Targets 6.0 (Chung, at el., 2006b) illustrates the use of the Star target and the Concentric Circle target, having varying line frequencies, to detect dot slur/doubling during printing. The effect of dot slur/doubling, captured by these targets, is mainly visual.

Dot slur/doubling causes excessive TVI variation in a pressrun. Being intermittent, dot slur/doubling is difficult to control during offset lithographic printing. The cure is not to adjust ink film thickness, but to find the root cause or leave it alone.

7.12. Process Capability and Process Improvement

In his book, *Understanding Variation, the Key to Managing Chaos*, Wheeler (1993) pointed out that (a) specifications (aims and tolerances) define the voice of the customer and do not describe the voice of the process, (b) data that have been digested and analyzed (averages, standard deviations) define the voice of the process, (c) process capability study involves the comparison of process data to specifications, and (d) one must understand how the inputs affect the outputs before one can improve the system.

When conducting a process capability study, samples are collected and measured. A normal distribution (or curve) is often the result of chance-caused variation (Figure 7.18). Characteristics of a normal curve include (a) process mean, median, and mode are at the center of the curve; (b) 68.3% of the population is within the ±1 standard deviation (s) around the process mean; (c) 95.4% of the population is within the ±2s around the process mean; and (d) 99.7% of the population is within the ±3s around the process mean (Rickmers and Todd, 1967).

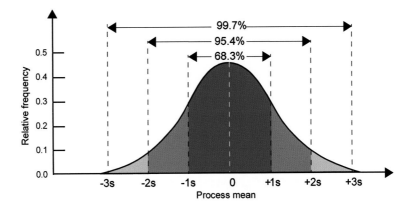

Figure 7.18.
A normal distribution
of 1-D data.

Printing-process control is about adjusting the process based on control limits, not tolerances. Process control limits (upper and lower control limits) come from process capability study. The upper control limit (UCL) is the process mean plus 3s, and the lower control limit (LCL) is the process mean minus 3s. The process mean (or production center) is computed using Eq. 7.3, and its standard deviation (s) is computed using Eq. 7.4.

$$X\_bar = \frac{\sum_{i=1}^{n} X_i}{n} \qquad \text{Eq. 7.3}$$

$$s = \sqrt{\frac{\sum_{i=1}^{n}(X_i - X\_bar)^2}{n-1}} \qquad \text{Eq. 7.4}$$

The parametric statistics work well for 1-D data (e.g., density). Although ΔE is 1-D, its distribution is, inherently, not normal, which makes statistical parameters, like standard deviation, less applicable. A different process control methodology is needed to work with 3-D data, such as CIELAB.

While printing-process control is based on control limits, process capability assessment is based on tolerance (DataMyte, 1989). For 1-D data, the process capability index (CP) assumes the centeredness of the process. and is the ratio between tolerance and process capability (6s), as shown in Eq. 7.5.

$$CP = \frac{\text{Tolerance}}{6\sigma} = \frac{USL - LSL}{6s} \qquad \text{Eq. 7.5}$$

A process is capable when CP > 1 (i.e., 6s is less than the tolerance). A process is not capable when CP ≤ 1 (i.e., 6s is equal to or greater than the tolerance).

For 1-D data, the process capability index (CpK) measures the performance of the process by taking into account both the spread of the distribution and where the distribution is. As shown in Eq. 7.6, CpK is the lesser of the two quantities in this equation. The following provides an example of calculating CP and CpK of a single-color printing process.

$$CpK = \text{The lesser of } \frac{(USL - \text{mean})}{3\sigma} \qquad \text{Eq. 7.6}$$

$$\text{or } \frac{(\text{mean} - LSL)}{3\sigma}$$

7.13. Case Study: Process Capability (CP and CpK)

The aim of the black solid ink density is 1.70 with a lower specification limit (LSL) of 1.60 and an upper specification limit (USL) of 1.80. Upon press sheet sampling, measurement, and data analysis, the mean value is 1.65 and the standard deviation (s) is 0.05.

Upon CP calculation, the black printer has more variation than the tolerance (CP index is less than 1 or 0.67).

$$CP = \frac{USL - LSL}{(6)(0.05)} = \frac{1.80 - 1.60}{0.3} = \frac{0.2}{0.3} = 0.67$$

Upon CpK calculation, the black printer performance was not centered (CpK index is 0.33). Figure 7.19 is a graphic depiction of the process capability study.

$$CpK = \text{Lesser of} \left[\frac{(USL - mean)}{3\sigma} \text{ or } \frac{(mean - LSL)}{3\sigma} \right]$$

$$= \text{Lesser of} \left[\frac{(1.80 - 1.65)}{(3)(0.05)} \text{ or } \frac{(1.65 - 1.60)}{(3)(0.05)} \right]$$

$$= \text{Lesser of} \left[\frac{0.15}{0.15} \text{ or } \frac{0.05}{0.15} \right]$$

$$= \text{Lesser of} [1.0 \text{ or } 0.33] = 0.33$$

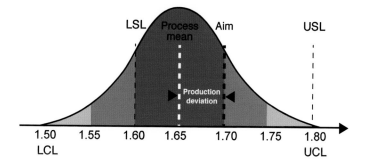

Figure 7.19.
Graphic depiction of the process capability study.

When CpK (0.33) is less than CP (0.67), this is a sign of production deviation or the misalignment between process mean and the aim. From a process improvement point of view, adjusting the process mean closer to the aim point, that is, increasing solid ink density by 0.05, is a quick data-driven decision.

7.14. Technological Advances and Process Automation

Automation is the result of technological advances that eliminate complex hand work and get the task done faster, better, and cheaper. Since the 1960s, technological advances in the typesetting industry have gone from hot-metal typesetting to phototypesetting to laser typesetting. Laser or digital imaging eventually combined typesetting and imagesetting in one operation.

Automation in the electronic color imaging industry began in 1979 with a company called Scitex, in Israel. It showed the Response system, the first color editing and retouching workstation that allowed color images to be changed in a matter of minutes instead of many hours of dot etching. Ten years later, a Mac and Adobe Photoshop replaced the

Scitex Response at only a fraction of the hardware and software costs.

Automation in offset printing became evident when computer-to-plate technology replaced film-based imagesetting and when new offset presses increased press speed, reduced makeready time, increased productivity with an automatic plate change-over, while blanket and rollers were washed simultaneously.

Process control includes color measurement, process monitoring, and adjustment. An off-line spectrophotometer is not robust enough for real-time process control during printing. An on-line closed-loop scanning spectrophotometer, for example, AVT/GMI Clarios, is capable of performing process control for a high-speed web press (Figure 7.20).

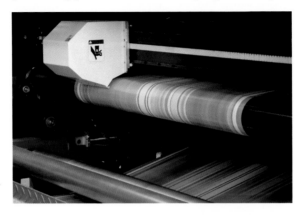

Figure 7.20.
Clarios on-line scanning spectropho-tometer. (Reprinted with permission from Advanced Vision Technology [AVT] Ltd.)

A closed-loop scanning spectrophotometer collects spectral color measurements on running webs, both across the web width and over time, and displays inking uniformity (Figure 7.21L) and consistency (Figure 7.21R) at top production speeds. It computes ISO 13655-compliant process control metrics, from basic solid ink density, TVI, and gray balance, to ΔE (ISO, 2009b). It also displays and controls inking of the printing units in real-time. All time-stamped color data are automatically saved and can be recalled for process capability studies and reported to the management.

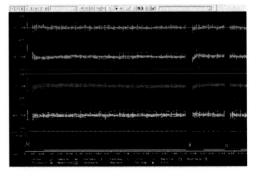

Figure 7.21.
Inking uniformity (left); inking consistency (right). (Reprinted with permission from Advanced Vision Technology [AVT] Ltd.)

Not only must sampling and measurement be timely, analyses and corrective actions of printing-process control must be sound. Closed-loop control applies modern control theory, that is, robotics and artificial intelligence (AI), for real-time diagnostics and adjustments without human intervention. Press operators can override the controls to handle exceptions.

7.15. Chapter Summary

Printing-process control begins with known materials and press calibration. We determine the calibration deviation by measuring press sheets at the beginning of the pressrun. We find out production deviation and production variation by measuring subsequent press sheets during the pressrun.

Sampling and measurements tend to fluctuate randomly when there is no adjustment made on press. When adjustments are made on press, for example, changes in ink film thickness, the impact on solid coloration is apparent. But, the impact on TVI, gray balance, and color image reproduction varies.

Printing-process control may be summarized by five action words: *Plan–Measure–Look–Think–Act*. *Plan* means you (1) know your process and printing specifications, including well-defined paper–ink–press conditions, and (2) understand that the press is the wrong place to perform color correction if it could have been done in prepress. In other words, color correction during printing cannot be done selectively to images as can color correction in prepress.

Measure means you (1) use instruments to collect color data from the color control bar and (2) use curved plates to achieve color, tone reproduction, or gray balance conformity during press calibration.

Look means you (1) examine image-to-image registration of printed color reproduction and (2) examine CMY triplets in relation to K tints during production runs. If there is gray mismatch, verify the mismatch visually and identify root causes before introducing corrective actions.

Think means you (1) understand that "print by number" is the new norm that replaces a customer's sign-off, and (2) use SPC tools to control the pressrun.

Finally, *Act* means you use measurement devices, including SPC tools and AI, to effectively control the printed color side to side and beginning to end effectively.

7.16. Multiple-Choice and Essay Questions

1. Regulating activities to verify the conformance of a process to a standard and to take corrective action, as needed, in a manufacturing is called _____.
A. printing certification
B. process control
C. printing audit
D. product inspection

2. In ISO 12647-2, the deviation tolerance is the permissive difference (ΔE, ΔTVI, midtone spread) between _____.
A. the average of all measurements and the aim values
B. the average of all measurements and the OK sheet
C. measurements from the OK sheet and the aim values
D. None of the above

3. Analyses of process control parameters, for example, CIELAB, TVI, are based on _____.
A. visual inspection of print defects
B. destructive chemical analyses
C. measurement from color control bars
D. measurement from image spots

4. _____ is a measure of acceptability based on specified aims and tolerances.
A. Gray reproduction
B. Dot slur/doubling
C. Conformity
D. Perfection

5. Which statement is incorrect?
A. Random variation can be controlled.
B. Frequent press starts/stops tend to exhibit excessive color variation.
C. Paper splicing in web offset printing is a specially caused variation.
D. Ink film thickness can be adjusted in an offset press.

6. _____ is affected by calibration, and _____ is affected by process control.
A. Density, color
B. Midtone spread, TVI
C. Production samples, OK print
D. Deviation, variation

7. Images with _____ benefit the most with a high GCR setting in terms of gray stability in presswork.
A. high chroma contents
B. high frequency contents
C. lots of highlights
D. lots of dark tones and near neutrals

8. Dot slur/doubling, often intermittent and directional, is caused by wavy papers, web tensions, ink back-trap in _____ printing.
A. inkjet
B. offset
C. flexo
D. electrophotographic

9. When printing to solid coloration aims, _____ can be used to predict the change in solid ink density that best matches the specified CIELAB values.
A. the Murray-Davies equation
B. tristimulus integration
C. Beer's law
D. None of the above

10. For high-volume printing, _____ is used not only to minimize visual impact of color shift during printing, but also for ink cost savings, because black ink costs less than chromatic inks.
A. light GCR
B. medium GCR
C. heavy GCR
D. None of the above

11. Point out the three steps to implementing printing-process control.

12. Explain the application of Beer's law in solid coloration adjustment on an analog press.

8 *Test Targets:*
A Teaching and Learning Journey

When studying printing-process control and color management, there are many questions to ask. For example: How do we describe the visual difference between two colors that are $5\Delta E^*_{ab}$ apart? How do we distinguish AM screening from FM screening? What is the effect of optically brightened substrates on printed color? How do we differentiate digital printing from offset printing? One way to answer these questions is to design and print a test form containing the subject matter of interest, perform color measurements, conduct visual examinations, and report the findings.

Print media, in the form of books, catalogs, magazines, and brochures, is used by publishers, advertisers, brands, and institutions to tell stories, sell products, and provide instruction. *Test Targets* is a print publication about printing-process control and color management. This chapter describes how *Test Targets* are used as a teaching and learning tool in an academic environment to answer questions concerning tone reproduction and color image reproduction.

8.1. Background of *Test Targets*

Before *Test Targets* was a reality, a student would pick a topic, do the experiment, use a color proofer to generate samples, design a poster, and make an oral presentation in the classroom. While this was a form of learning by doing, students in the class and the instructor were the only audience.

Two technological breakthroughs in the 1990s made *Test Targets* publication possible. The first breakthrough was the introduction of a desktop-based ICC color-management system that replaced the proprietary color electronic prepress system. The second breakthrough was the introduction of digital printing systems capable of short-run printing directly from digital files. We could manipulate color settings in prepress, experiment with different press calibration methods, measure and analyze printed color reproduction, and produce a publication within the school calendar and budget.

A scholarly publication should demonstrate its technical contents through good writing skills. Edline Chun, who taught the *Technical*

Report Writing course, conducted writing workshops for student authors. She emphasized that the abstract should be concise; the introduction should cover the scope of the work; literature review should provide a conceptual framework; and the bibliography should follow an agreed-upon style (Chung et al., 2004). Later, Edline Chun became the chief editor of *Test Targets* publications.

8.2. *Test Targets* Requirements

Test Targets requirements fall within the following six areas: content, format, authors, review, print production, and distribution.

1. Content

From a printing-process control point of view, *Test Targets* content should include (a) digital test targets as input to a color reproduction workflow; (b) prepress and color-management software to transform digital data to pixels; (c) printing devices to convert pixels into inked dots; and (d) color-measurement instruments and data analysis software to measure and analyze print samples.

From a research point of view, *Test Targets* content should include (a) test elements representing input to a printing process; (b) methods of altering certain independent variables (e.g., resolution, screening, solid coloration) to observe dependent variables, including visual and quantitative aspects of tone and color reproduction; and (c) printed color reproduction that documents insights into device characteristics and printing-process control.

2. Format

The publication is organized into three sections: (a) the front matter, which includes a title page, table of contents, and foreword; (b) the body text, which includes the topic, author, abstract, introduction, review of the literature, methods, results, acknowledgments, and references; and (c) the back matter, which includes the acknowledgments, author biographies, imposition, and pressrun organizers.

The body of the publication is further divided into three sections: (a) technical papers to document case studies; (b) test forms to showcase different test patterns of interest (e.g., how legacy CMYK files are rendered differently by different ink–substrate–press conditions); and (c) *Gallery of Visual Interest* (GVI) to make each publication more appealing by capturing interesting visual phenomena. For example, how to make one color look like two colors (see section 2.23, simultaneous contrast), and how to make two stimuli look like one color (see section 2.14, "Spectral Match and Metameric Match").

3. Authors

Test Targets are authored by three groups, student, faculty, and alumni, sometimes in collaboration. Student authors are those who enroll in Printing Process Control class and Advanced Color Management class. Faculty authors are instructors of the technical courses and the Technical Report Writing course. Alumni authors are former students. Figure 8.1 is a group photo of students and faculty members in the courtyard of the College of Imaging Arts and Sciences (now College of Art and Design) in 2004.

Figure 8.1.
A group photo of students and faculty *Test Targets* authors in 2004.

4. Review

Review is a necessary part of the learning process. Multiple reviews are deemed necessary. The first level is peer review, that is, a student author reviews another student author's work. The second level is technical review by faculty members. The third level is editorial review. Edline Chun, who taught Technical Report Writing, ensured correct use of English language and used Track Changes to show the students how to write the paper.

5. Print Production

Design and prepress are handled by student authors. Microsoft Word is used as the writer's tool. Adobe InDesign is used as the pagination and imposition tool.

Press Run Organizer (PRO), like a job ticket, is a communication tool between content and print media. It organizes information in terms of the content to be printed, medium, screening, ink, and paper. PRO also specifies signature, imposition, printing, and quantities. We created a PRO for each printing device used.

Printing is done by technicians in the School of Media Sciences Laboratory and Printing Applications Laboratory at RIT. During press-runs, students perform sampling and color measurement on site.

6. Distribution

Some hard copies of *Test Targets* are available at RIT Press, http://ritpress. rit.edu/. Digital versions of *Test Targets* (PDF) are available online at RIT Scholar Works (http://scholarworks.rit.edu). Use the advanced search, that is, search by title (test targets) and limit the search (books), to identify *Test Targets* publications.

8.3.   *Test Targets* Publications at a Glance

Table 8.1 provides an overview of *Test Targets,* published from 2002 to 2011, in chronological order. For each issue, the publication date, page count, press used to print the cover, and press used to print the body of the text block, are listed. *Test Targets* covers were typically printed using the Heidelberg Speedmaster 74 sheetfed offset press on 100 lb cover stock. *Test Targets* text blocks were typically printed with sheetfed and web offset presses. Occasionally, a digital production press and a sheetfed offset press were benchmarked for print-quality purposes. *Test Targets* finishing was outsourced to a local Smyth-sewn book bindery.

Table 8.1. *Test Targets* publications at a glance.

Publication	Date of issue	No. of pages	Body text printed by	Cover printed by
Test Targets 2.0	June 2002	34	Indigo UltraStream 2000	Indigo UltraStream
Test Targets 3.0	March 2003	40	Heidelberg M-1000B	Heidelberg SM74
Test Targets 3.1	July 2003	64	Heidelberg Sunday 2000	Heidelberg SM74
Test Targets 4.0	June 2004	80	Heidelberg Sunday 2000	Heidelberg SM74
Test Targets 5.0	Dec. 2005	80	Kodak NexPress 2100	Heidelberg SM74
Test Targets 6.0	Nov. 2006	80	Heidelberg SM74 + EK NexPress	Heidelberg SM74
Test Targets 7.0	Nov. 2007	88	Sunday 2000 + NexPress	Heidelberg SM74
Test Targets 8.0	Nov. 2008	96	Heidelberg SM74 + Indigo 5500	Heidelberg SM74
Test Targets 9.0	Nov. 2009	88	Heidelberg SM74 + EK Prosper 5000XL	Heidelberg SM74
Test Targets 10	Nov. 2011	84	Sunday 2000	HP Indigo 7000

From 2002 to 2011, the RIT School of Media Sciences published 10 *Test Targets* monographs. A total of 91 technical papers were authored by 40 student authors, 4 faculty authors, 5 alumni authors, and 3 visiting scholars.

Table 8.2 provides a list of *Test Targets* collaborators. The supply side of the graphic arts industry was very supportive of *Test Targets*. Paper companies provided us with rolls and skids of papers; ink companies provided us with standard process inks, Pantone inks, and metallic inks; and software companies donated their color-management software packages. In addition, many industry professionals donated their time and energies to review *Test Targets* papers.

Table 8.2. *Test Targets* collaborators.

Company	Product
Alwan	Alwan ColorHub
bvdm	Roman 16 Reference Images
ChroMix	ColorThink Pro
Color Logic	MetalFX Inks
Eastman Kodak	Proper 5000XL Inkjet Press
Eckart	MetalStar NL-Silver
Iggesund Paperboard	Invercote T & G
Sappi	Sappi McCoy
Superior Printing Inks	Spot color inks
X-Rite	i1 iSis Spectrophotometer

Below are highlights of each publication. The inaugural issue, *Test Targets 2.0*, was printed in 2002. Incidentally, *Test Targets 1.0* does not exist.

8.4. *Test Targets 2.0* and the Indigo UltraStream 2000 Digital Press

Test Targets 2.0 was a 34-page publication. Both the text block and the cover of *Test Targets 2.0* were printed by the Indigo UltraStream 2000 digital press (Chung et al., 2002). As shown in Figure 8.2 (left), it has an interesting cover design—a color chart when viewed up close, but the words "TEST TARGETS" jump out of the color chart when viewed from a distance.

The Indigo UltraStream 2000 is an electrophotographic printing press, capable of four-color printing at the speed of 2000 impressions per hour. It was the first digital printing system in the school capable of printing 12 in. × 18 in. sheets or 4-page signatures. We wrote about the nomenclature of digital test forms and print-quality assessment by densitometry and by colorimetry.

As shown in Figure 8.2 (center), a technical paper shows the effect of TVI change on tone and color reproduction and the use of 1-D transfer curves to match different output devices due to TVI differences. Figure 8.2 (right) also demonstrates the effect of digital camera profiling on color image reproductions of oil paintings.

Figure 8.2.
Test Targets 2.0 cover and sample pages.

8.5. *Test Targets 3.0* and the Growing Pains of Color Management

Test Targets 3.0 (Chung et al., 2003a) was a 40-page publication (Figure 8.3). The text block of *Test Targets 3.0* was printed using the Heidelberg M-1000B web offset press. Its cover was printed using the Heidelberg Speedmaster 74 (SM74) sheetfed offset press.

 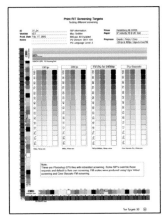 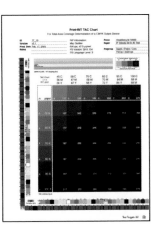

Figure 8.3.

Test Targets 3.0 cover and sample pages.

The SM74 is a sheetfed offset press capable of printing 360 ft/min (1200 sheets/hr). The sheet size is 4 letter-size pages or an 8-page signature. Assuming that the printing nip is 10 cm (0.4 in.) wide, the ink-and-paper contact duration at the printing nip is 0.005 sec.

The M-1000B is a web offset press capable of printing 1000 ft/min (30,000 sheets/hr). The sheet size is 8 letter-size pages or a 16-page signature. Assuming that the printing nip is also 10 cm (0.4 in.) wide, the ink-and-paper contact duration at the nip is 0.002 sec.

The SM74 prints one side at a time, whereas the M-1000B prints both sides of the paper simultaneously, also known as "perfecting." The productivity ratio (square feet/time) between a sheetfed offset and a web offset press is 1:10.

Test Targets 3.0 captured the growing pains of color-management technology. Back in 2003, printer profiling required significant resources: a printer profiling target, no fewer than two pressruns with ink and paper consumables, a color-measurement instrument, and profiling software.

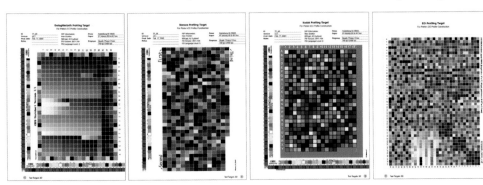

Figure 8.4.

Different proprietary printer profiling targets.

There was no standard profiling target then. Color-management software vendors had to create and promote their own printer profiling targets, which took up a lot of valuable press resources (Figure 8.4).

It was a breakthrough when the printer profiling target was standardized by ISO 12642-2 (IT8.7/4) in 2005 (Figure 8.5) with two suggested patch layouts: visual and random.

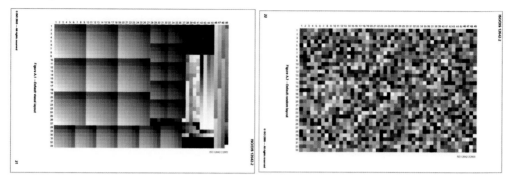

Test Targets 3.0 was the last pressrun of the M-1000B web offset press at RIT before it was dismantled and shipped elsewhere.

8.6. *Test Targets 3.1* and the Heidelberg Sunday 2000 Web Offset Press

The Heidelberg Sunday 2000 web offset press, printing at the speed of 2000 ft/min using gapless blanket cylinders, was a new addition to the RIT campus in 2003. The *Test Targets* group could not have been more thrilled, and we produced *Test Targets 3.1* to check out capabilities of the new press.

Test Targets 3.1 (Chung et al., 2003b) was a 64-page publication. Figure 8.6 shows its cover, and the class in front of the new Sunday 2000 press. The panoramic view of the press was captured by using a digital camera mounted on a tripod with a pano-head controlling leveling and rotation, followed by stitching six images together in Adobe Photoshop.

Lingjun Kong, a visiting scholar from Shanghai, China, investigated the effect of substrate backing on three different ink–paper–press combinations and tested the spectral-based correction algorithm proposed by Hans Ott. A student author investigated the role of image content on objective color image matching. Another student author conducted a colorimetric analysis of color image reproduction.

Figure 8.5.
ISO 12642-2 printer profiling targets (visual, random). (Reproduced with permission from ANSI on behalf of ISO. All rights reserved.)

Figure 8.6.
Test Targets 3.1 cover and group photo.

8.7. *Test Targets 4.0* and Hexachrome FM Screening

Test Targets 4.0 (Chung et al., 2004) was an 80-page publication. We embarked on extended-gamut research by printing the cover with a six-color Hexachrome and FM screening using the Heidelberg Speedmaster 74 sheetfed press (Figure 8.7, left). The body of the publication was printed using the Heidelberg Sunday 2000 web offset press.

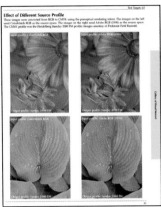

Figure 8.7.

Test Targets 4.0 cover and sample pages.

Figure 8.7 (center) illustrates the effect of different RGB profiles on printed color reproduction. A student author assessed watercolor reproduction quantitatively (Figure 8.7, right). The second student author compared color reproduction using a Hexachrome and CMYK. A third student author compared the effect of AM and FM screening on dot gain and how to compensate dot gain to achieve the same tone reproduction. The fourth student author assessed and compared process capability of the Xerox DocuColor 2060, a digital printer, and the Sunday 2000 web offset press.

Franz Sigg conducted a quantitative comparison of color differences. He demonstrated the use of an Excel template by graphing ΔE^*_{ab} and ΔE_{00} distributions, including CRF. Today, the 95th percentile ΔE^*_{ab} and ΔE_{00}, depicted from the color characterization target, are used as the tolerance metric in assessing color conformity in the ISO/PAS 15339-1 printing standards (ISO/PAS, 2015c).

8.8. *Test Targets 5.0* and the NexPress 2100 Electro-photographic Digital Press

Test Targets 5.0 (Chung et al., 2005) was an 80-page publication. The cover was printed using a Heidelberg Speedmaster sheetfed offset press, and the text block was printed using a NexPress 2100 digital press. Figure 8.8 illustrates the *Test Targets 5.0* cover and two sample pages regarding single black, rich black, and GCR.

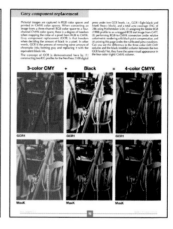

While toner-based digital color printing systems can match the color appearance of offset lithography, there is a productivity difference between the two printing technologies. To explain, a Sunday 2000 web offset press was used to print *Test Targets 4.0*. Each signature is 16 pages. The top press speed of the Sunday 2000 is 2000 ft/min or about 1000 impressions/min. The production of a 76-page publication for a quantity of 2000 copies takes less than half a day. In contrast, the NexPress 2100 digital press was used to print *Test Targets 5.0*. Each signature is 4 pages, and the top press speed of NexPress 2100 is 100 impressions/min. The production of a 76-page publication for a quantity of 2000 copies is five 8-hr days. So there is a factor of 10× in printing speed and 4× in area coverage, or a factor of 40× in productivity difference between the two printing technologies. This is why web offset printing is ideal for long-run publication printing, and digital printing is suitable for on-demand, short-run, and variable-data printing.

A student author investigated PDF/X workflows for the graphic arts industry. Another student author tested device-link profiling. Franz Sigg wrote his personal story, *Film-based Targets, the End of an Era*. It was about his family's printing business, where lithography had been accomplished since the 1930s with the use of limestone blocks, and his own professional life, which had been centered on film-based test target design and manufacturing since 1960. After 45 years of film-based target manufacturing, he was forced to close his business, which could not compete in the new digital era. Through his story, we learned that printing technology is a continuum, and we need to adopt new technologies to be successful.

Figure 8.8.

Test Targets 5.0 cover and sample pages.

8.9. *Test Targets 6.0* and the Gallery of Visual Interest (GVI)

Test Targets 6.0 (Chung et al., 2006b) was an 80-page publication. Figure 8.9 (left) illustrates its cover design, adopted from the RIT Concentric Circle and printed with metallic silver inks on the Heidelberg Speedmaster sheetfed press.

 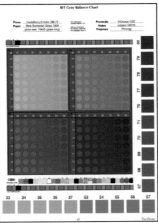 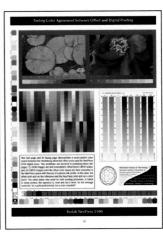

Figure 8.9.

Test Targets 6.0 cover and sample pages.

Figure 8.9 (center) showcases the RIT gray balance chart, a method to define cyan, magenta, and yellow dot areas required to achieve neutrality and tone reproduction for an ink–paper–press condition. This is in contrast to the G7 method, whereby a set of predetermined CMY triplets, upon printing and tonal adjustments, produce neutrals. In addition, the metameric match between a 3-color gray patch and a black-only patch makes an excellent laboratory resource.

An alumnus authored the paper, *Matching Electrophotographic Color Printing to Offset Lithography—Color Measurement Targets Perform Magic,* and used the test form, Figure 8.9 (right), printed as a 2-page spread to demonstrate color match between a Kodak NexPress digital color press and a Heidelberg sheetfed offset press. The visual match was spot-on; the difference could be discovered only in the resolution of the two printing devices, as evidenced in micro-type reproduction.

When ISO 12647-2 specified $5\Delta E^*_{ab}$ as the permissible color difference in process color printing, people began to wonder about the connection between "color difference by numbers" and "visual sensation." To answer this question, GVI demonstrates the visual difference by printing five color pairs that are approximately $5\Delta E^*_{ab}$ apart. Many industry consultants and trainers were pleased to have the "color difference by numbers" visual as a teaching aid.

Bit depth, resolution, color space, and image size define the file size of pictorial color image data. GVI illustrates visual differences of a test image from 8 bit to 7 bit, 6 bit, and so on. A 1 bit per pixel image is line art; an image with 2 or 3 bits per pixel is posterized; at 4 or more bits per pixel an image starts to look like a continuous-tone image. This is where many digital printing systems would lower the bit depth of the job data to optimize their printing performance without compromising image quality.

A student author explored process control in metallic color printing using commonly available color-measurement methods. An alumnus author investigated the effect of the continuous dampening system on color consistency of a sheetfed offset press.

Franz Sigg described the use of the RIT Contrast-Resolution Target for assessing resolution and contrast of an imaging system. Today, ISO/PDTS 18621-31.4 (ISO, 2018b), documenting the evaluation of the perceived resolution of printing systems with the contrast-resolution chart, is based on his research, published in *Test Targets 6.0*.

8.10. *Test Targets 7.0* and Printing-Process Control

Test Targets 7.0 (Chung et al., 2007) was an 88-page publication. Its text block was printed using a Heidelberg Sunday 2000 web offset press. Its cover was printed using a Heidelberg Speedmaster 74 sheetfed offset press. The cover, as shown in Figure 8.10 (left), has a magenta disk that appears to have the same color clockwise until it reaches to the twelve o'clock position. It points out the importance of spatial uniformity of inking, especially in packaging printing. Figure 8.10 (right) illustrates the challenges of panoramic photography and cross-signature color match using different screening technologies.

 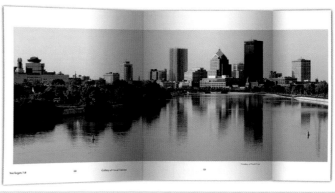

Franz Sigg described how to generate a custom test wedge in the form of an EPS file using a Microsoft Excel template. The author of this volume investigated the use of colorimetry to implement printing-process control by examining the performance of three process control metrics, ΔD_T, ΔD_λ, and ΔC^*, when controlling thicknesses of cyan, magenta, and yellow solid ink film. D_T is the traditional Status T density; D_λ is the spectral density of the maximum absorption of the ink; and C^* is the metric chroma of the ink. The results showed that there was no single metric that performs significantly better than other metrics. Wuhui Liu, a visiting scholar from Wuhan, China, coauthored a paper with the author of this volume on achieving color agreement using different color-adjustment methods. The three digital data adjustment methods they tested in 2007 were the device calibration techniques described in ISO/TS 10128 (ISO, 2015a).

Figure 8.10.
Test Targets 7.0 cover and sample foldout.

8.11. *Test Targets 8.0* and the HP Indigo 5500 Electro-photographic Digital Press

Test Targets 8.0 (Chung et al., 2008) was a 96-page publication. Both the body text and the cover were printed using a Heidelberg Speedmaster SM74 sheetfed offset press. Figure 8.11 (left) illustrates the cover, printed using the MetalFX ink system. The body text was printed using the SM74 or HP Indigo 5500 digital printing system.

   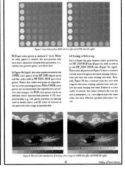

Figure 8.11.

Test Targets 8.0 cover and sample pages.

Test Forms—The ink sequence test form, as shown in Figure 8.11 (center-left), captures the effect of the ink sequence, CMYK versus KCMY, on offset printing using a specially designed test target. The spot color overprint test form captures the effect of overprint color, based on two spot color inks and the ink sequence.

GVI—This is a hard-to-find visual comparison of pictorial color image reproduction using red, green, and blue inks as primaries, as shown in Figure 8.11 (center-right and right), versus using CMYK inks. The next piece shows the design and printing with the MetalFX system. In addition, Lissajous figures illustrate spiral traces or oscillations of mathematical formulas.

Technical Papers—The HP Indigo 5500 digital press is a seven-color printing system. The author of this volume demonstrated the pictorial color image reproduction using red, green, and blue inks via multichannel ICC profiles and explained why CMYK inks are the choice for primaries in pictorial color reproduction. Michael Riordan, a faculty member, reported on design and printing with the MetalFX System. A student author described two approaches, a look-up table and a spectral-based model, to predict the color of spot color overprinting.

8.12. *Test Targets 9.0* and the Kodak Proper 5000XL Production Inkjet Press

Test Targets 9.0 (Chung et al., 2009) was an 88-page publication. The cover, Figure 8.12 (left), was printed using a Heidelberg Speedmaster 74 sheet-fed offset press and the text block was printed using an SM74 or a Kodak Proper 5000XL high-speed inkjet press.

Figure 8.12 (center) illustrates the use of a test form to analyze visual color match between the new high-speed Proper 5000XL production inkjet press and the commercial sheetfed offset benchmark. Figure 8.12 (right) illustrates the use of low-key pictorial color images to study the use of GCR for ink savings in the pressroom.

Figure 8.12.
Test Targets 9.0 cover and sample pages.

Technical Papers—A student author tackled two problems relating to color perception and color measurement: "What quantitative metrics correlate with pleasing visuals?" and "What quantitative metrics correlate with color image match?" She output three pictorial images to four printing devices (sheetfed offset, drop-on-demand inkjet, continuous inkjet, and electrophotography) in two conditions: (1) printing to the full gamut of the device, and (2) printing to match the reference (sheetfed offset) device. Based on the paired comparison tests with seven observers, she concluded that (1) there is a correlation between addressability and pleasing visuals, that is, fine detail is an attribute of a pleasing image; and (2) the smaller the ΔE^*_{ab} among selected color swatches, the better the visual match.

Three papers were related to ISO standards. The author of this volume wrote a paper, "International Printing Standards, a Value-added Proposition." He coauthored a case study with Fred Hsu, RIT Printing Applications Laboratory, "Assessing Printing Process Conformance According to ISO 12647-2." A student author reported on image quality assessment according to ISO 13660 (ISO, 2001) and ISO 19751 (ISO, 2004).

A student author assessed the performance of four color-difference equations. He prepared test samples from the Pantone swatch book, having at least four Pantone colors with a color difference of $6\Delta E^*_{ab}$ to 10 reference Pantone colors. The results showed that ΔE_{DIN99} had the highest agreement with visual judgments, and this was followed by ΔE_{CMC}, ΔE_{00}, ΔE^*_{ab}, and finally ΔE_{94}.

8.13. *Test Targets 10* and Optical Brightening Agents

Test Targets 10 (Chung et al., 2010) was an 84-page publication, with its text block printed using a Goss Sunday 2000 web offset press, and its cover printed using a HP Indigo 7000 digital press. Figure 8.13 (left) illustrates its cover and sample pages. Figure 8.13 (center) are Roman 16 Reference Images, and Figure 8.13 (right) is a test page to show side-by-side visual comparison of pictorial and synthetic color images printed on paper with and without an OBA.

Figure 8.13.

Test Targets 10 cover and sample pages.

Technical Papers—Two papers focused on printing standardization and conformity assessment. Pierre Urbain, a student author, coauthored a paper with Elie Khoury, Alwan, that described data-reception requirements in ISO 12647-2 (ISO, 2013a) and ISO 15930 (2007b). They also demonstrated the use of a test PDF file to assess conformity of any PDF workflow. The author of this volume described aims and tolerances specified in ISO 12647-2 and the use of color measurement and data analysis tools for conformity assessment. Ivy Tian, a visiting scholar from Shanghai, China, coauthored a paper with the author of this volume describing the effect of paper containing OBA on printed colors. They showed how such quantitative differences could be reconciled using different mathematical models. Scott Millward, a student author, and Franz Sigg coauthored a paper reporting the stability of OBA as a function of exposure over time.

8.14. Chapter Summary

From a teaching and learning point of view, there is a significant difference between a lab assignment and a publication. In a lab assignment, students go through the hands-on portion of the lab and report their lab findings. In a publication, student authors have to select their technical topics, define the procedures, carry out the experiments, and document major findings. Students expressed excitement at being first-time authors and noted the value of including a publication on their résumés.

Test Targets has been a source of inspiration that drives students and faculty members to be innovative. Those who have engaged in content creation and production management realize that this is hard work. But there is a strong sense of gratification when the publication is held in one's hands, fresh off the press. This, in turn, creates an urge to repeat that experience.

Test Targets has become a collectable among printing students and industry professionals. One issue may contain topics in process control and color management with specific findings. Another issue may contain printing standardization and associated case studies. Seeing is believing—the GVI illustrates digital printing versus offset printing, AM screening versus FM screening, and the effect of an OBA on printed color. This is another reason that people collect *Test Targets*.

Test Targets had a terrific run of 10 years (2002—2011). The publication was dormant from 2012 to 2016 due to a change of teaching and research focus, followed by faculty retirement. The Sunday 2000 web offset press at RIT also had a terrific run of 10 years (2003—2013) before being dismantled in 2013.

A good idea is worth continuing. In 2017, *Test Targets 11* was published by Bruce Myers, faculty member, and his students at RIT School of Media Sciences. The publication continues the tradition of diffusing research conducted in the school while simultaneously teaching students print production principles and skills.

8.15. Multiple-Choice and Essay Questions

1. A series of fine-line and fine-dot patterns are characteristics of a _____ target.
A. gray balance
B. resolution
C. dot slur and doubling
D. device profiling

2. A C50M40Y40 gray patch, plus a matching black tint, is a useful target for assessing _____ in process color printing.
A. resolution
B. color variation
C. dot doubling
D. screening

3. Unlike job data, test targets represent _____ in graphic arts imaging.
A. specific file format
B. known input values
C. proprietary algorithm
D. customer jobs

4. Having two identical test targets, e.g., two IT8.7/4, situated in different orientation in a test form is useful to _____.
A. assess temporal consistency
B. assess spatial uniformity
C. meet profiling requirement
D. fill up the extra space

5. The IT8.7/4 target _____.
A. has 1617 color patches
B. contains all color patches in the ISO 12642-2
C. is a color characterization target for process color printing
D. All of the above

6. A red rose, printed using _____, is an excellent subject to demonstrate visual impact of the extended color gamut.

A. a flexographic press
B. a web offset press
C. a high-speed inkjet press
D. Hexachrome and FM screening

7. When using red, green, and blue inks to reproduce a pictorial color image on paper, _____ is absent in its color gamut.

A. gray
B. black
C. yellow
D. blue

8. _____ can be used to study the relationship between quantitative color difference and visual color difference.

A. Color pairs
B. Images with low GCR and high GCR
C. AM and FM screening
D. OBA and non-OBA substrate

9. "Make one color looks like two colors" is a visual phenomenon called _____.

A. color constancy
B. chromatic adaptation
C. simultaneous contrast
D. tristimulus integration

10. "Make two stimuli look like one color" is an interaction between light and color, called _____.

A. color constancy
B. chromatic adaptation
C. simultaneous contrast
D. illuminant metamerism

11. Why are cyan, magenta, and yellow inks used in process color printing, and not red, green, and blue inks?

12. Why is a 150 lpi AM halftone screen a de facto standard for commercial printing?

9 Printing Standards in a Changing Industry

There are two forces of change in the printing industry: technology push and demand pull. Between technology push and demand pull, new printing standards are developed and existing standards are revised to ensure that print buyers' needs are met and the printing industry stays viable and competitive. Printing standards embody technologies, markets, guidelines, and requirements. Unless a person is intimately involved in the standard development process, it is difficult to understand what new standards are and why existing standards require revision. This chapter looks at technology push, demand pull, and their impacts on new printing standards development, including ISO/TS 15311-1 digital printing standard (ISO, 2018a); proof–print match, ISO/PAS 15339-1 (ISO, 2015c); and CGATS TR 016 (2012, 2014) multilevel tolerance for data set conformity. This chapter also looks at how existing standards, for example, ISO 13655 (ISO, 2009c) and ISO 3664 (ISO, 2009a), are revised to better meet the color measurement and viewing needs of the industry.

9.1. Demand Pull

Print buyers are important stakeholders in the printing industry. They are aware of the value of printing standards. They specify printing requirements. They demand printing quality. They are satisfied when printing quality standards are met. They will complain when printing or service quality standards are not met.

Preference is a choice in decision-making. Clean and bright color reproduction has been print buyers' color preference. This is why printing standards were developed, at some point, to address such needs, including paper specifications. But clean and bright color reproduction (e.g., whiter whites or redder reds) can be a moving target when print buyers demand more choices. This is why standards must evolve to address the print buyers' changing needs.

9.2. Technology Push

Digital imaging has been the driver for creating the graphic arts prepress standards. For example, the standard in the 1980s, the Digital Data Exchange Standard (DDES), defined image data structures to be portable and exchangeable among color electronic prepress systems (CEPS); the standard in the 1990s, CGATS TR 001 (CGATS, 1995), defined not only the data (dot area of CMYK separation), but also how it should be specified in the web offset publication printing industry (SWOP). In a sense, SWOP was the precursor to ISO-sanctioned CRPCs.

As desktop systems replaced the high-end CEPS in the 2000s, Adobe's PDF/X or ISO 15930-7 (ISO, 2007b) integrated texts, vector graphics, and images in a single document. PDF/X provides not only a data-exchange format, but also the ICC profile to specify the intended printing conditions within the file. Today, digital printing is the driver for the next wave of graphic arts standards.

Digital printing technology uses electro-photographic or inkjet, instead of offset, gravure, and flexography, to reproduce fixed or variable data as hard copy. As shown in Table 9.1, PDF/X (ISO 15930-7) applies to both analog and digital printing technologies. Process control parameters and visual characteristics of digital printing are broader in scope than those of analog printing. ISO 12647, a series of standards developed for analog printing technology, no longer suffice for digital printing. ISO/PAS 15339-1 and ISO/TS 15311 (ISO, 2018a) are the results of digital printing standards development in ISO/TC 130. ISO/PAS 15339 has been introduced in chapter 4, section 4.15. Below is an introduction to ISO/TS 15311-1: Digital Printing Standard.

Table 9.1. Analog and digital printing workflow and standards.

Stage	Analog printing	Digital printing
Document design	ISO 15930	
Concept proof	ISO 12647-8	
Contract proof	ISO 12647-7	----
Printing	ISO 12647 series	ISO/PAS 15339 ISO/TS 15311
Finishing	----	----

9.3.   ISO/TS 15311-1: Digital Printing Standard

The advancement of digital printing technology drives the development of ISO/TS 15311, *Graphic Technology—Print Quality Requirements for Printed Matter*. Part 1 of the standard is *Measurement Methods and Reporting Schema* (ISO, 2018a). The standard defines print-quality metrics, measurement methods, and reporting requirements for printed sheets that are suitable for all classes of printed products.

Because process control parameters and visual characteristics of digital printing and analog printing processes are different, this technical specification is aimed at specifying a minimum set of parameters that define the visual characteristics and technical properties of digital printed products. These parameters include the following seven aspects:

1. Printing aim: ISO/TS 15311-1 assumes that the printing aim is a reference characterization data set, which may mimic a conventional printing process or match an agreed-upon characterization data set used in digital printing applications.

2. Color accuracy: Color accuracy describes the visual closeness between a defined reference and a reproduction. ISO/TS 15311-1 defines absolute and media-relative color accuracy. Absolute color accuracy applies to side-by-side or simultaneous viewing of two objects; and media-relative color accuracy is suitable for stand-alone viewing of a single object.

3. Color variation: Color variation describes color differences between the mean of a set of color measurements and each sample. It applies to production variation (also see chapter 7, section 7.2). It does not involve the OK print, as specified in ISO 12647-2.

4. Sampling: The number of sheets to be measured depends on the run length, but should not exceed 15 samples.

5. Gloss: The gloss of substrate and solid tone colors of the sample should be visually similar to the reference print to be simulated.

6. Uniformity: This refers to the color nonuniformity across a large image area that is intended to be uniform. The lack of uniformity may be due to various artifacts, such as banding, mottling, graininess, show-through, edge-to-edge nonuniformity, and so on.

7. Other requirements: Depending on use cases, resolution, artifacts, permanence, light fastness, or rub resistance are of importance.

To dovetail printing technology standards with conformity assessment guidelines, future revision of ISO/TS 15311-1 should adopt the same terminology and reporting requirements used in ISO/IEC 17067. Specifically, calibration deviation, production deviation, and production variation should be clearly defined.

9.4. Proof–Print Match, Past

In addition to clean and bright color, print buyers also demand proof–print match. Due to technology pushes, the solution to proof–print match has changed drastically over time. In the 1960s, press proofs were produced using production ink and paper on a sheetfed press. Producing press proofs was expensive and time-consuming. Film-based photomechanical proofs (e.g., DuPont Cromalin and 3M Matchprint) became viable alternatives from 1980 to 2000. These proofs were designed to simulate only one printing condition, SWOP (CGATS TR 001).

Since 2000, a number of reference printing conditions were registered in the ICC Profile Registry. It is the job of the digital proofing provider to simulate a specified reference printing condition using a color-managed inkjet proofing system; and the job of the printer is to print to the same reference printing condition. Thus, the relationship between proofing and printing has changed from *print to match a proof* in the past to *print and proof to match a characterization data set* (Chung et al., 2017). Regardless, proof–print match remains as a print buyer's demand.

With the blessing of metamerism and color management, print buyers accepted digital proofs, made from inkjet printers using standard proofing stocks to simulate the white point of the standard printing stock. This is why ISO 12647-2 (ISO, 2013a) specifies the color of the printing substrates, and ISO 12647-7 (ISO, 2015b) specifies that the white point of the proof must matches the white point of the printing condition.

9.5. Proof–Print Match, Today

Since 2010, print buyers have demanded nonstandard substrates containing varying amounts of OBA and expect the digital proofs and the prints, when viewed simultaneously, to match each other.

Today, there are too many printing substrates with varying OBA amounts. Proofing substrates manufacturers can no longer match OBA-loaded printing substrates. Proof–print match suffers. Printing conformity is in chaos because the substrate color difference alone exceeds the tolerance limits before printing begins.

Print buyers have the right to specify printing and proofing requirements. When color proofs no longer match OBA-loaded prints, they complain and demand a solution. The ISO/TC 130 attempted to revise the aim points and tolerances of paper specifications. But no consensus was reached due to different geographic preferences.

9.6. ISO/PAS 15339-1 and Proof–Print Match

The development of the ISO/PAS 15339-1 (ISO, 2015c) offered a proof–print match solution despite nonstandard printing substrates. The basic steps to implement the 15339-1 workflow are outlined below:

1. The designer/client picks a CRPC as the reference printing condition, a substrate, and a process for print production.

2. If the substrate color is the same as the CRPC white point, proof and print to the CRPC aims; else, proof and print to the SCCA (substrate-corrected colorimetric aims).

3. Printing-process control is the responsibility of the printer.

The next section describes the SCCA mechanism. It is followed by three case studies regarding printing and proofing to SCCA aims.

9.7. What's SCCA?

SCCA (substrate-corrected colorimetric aims), based on the tristimulus linear method, was first used to correct measurement backing difference (McDowell et al., 2005). The method was adopted by ISO 13655 (ISO, 2009b). Upon further testing, the method worked equally well for changes in substrate resulting from a basic shade change or a change in the OBA level (McDowell, 2012).

Equation 9.1 takes the form of a straight line, where the quantity, $(1 + C)$, is the slope and the quantity, $(X_{min}C)$, is the intercept.

$$X_2 = X_1(1 + C) - X_{min}C \qquad \text{Eq. 9.1}$$

$$C = \frac{X_{w2} - X_{w1}}{X_{w1} - X_{min}} \qquad \text{Eq. 9.2}$$

X_1 is the tristimulus value (X, Y, Z) of printed color on Substrate_1, X_2 is the corrected tristimulus value (X, Y, Z) of printed color on Substrate_2, (1 + C) is a constant, X_{w1} is the measured tristimulus value (X, Y, Z) of Substrate_1 (w1), and X_{w2} is the measured tristimulus value (X, Y, Z) of Substrate_2 (w2).

In a nutshell, substrate correction reconciles color differences between the production paper-based color gamut and the CRPC white point-based color gamut.

9.8. SCCA Calculation

One may develop a spreadsheet to perform the SCCA calculation by using the following steps:

1. Identify the target data set and CIELAB values of Substrate_1 and the maximum black of Substrate_1.

2. Identify CIELAB values of Substrate_2.

3. Convert the constants (X_{w1}, X_{min}, X_{w2}) and the target data set from CIELAB to CIEXYZ.

4. Compute the substrate-corrected CIEXYZ values using Equations 9.1 and 9.2.

5. Convert the substrate-corrected data set from CIEXYZ back to CIELAB.

Figure 9.1 is an example of the linear correction described in step 4. The x-axis represents the tristimulus values, X, Y, and Z of the target data set. The y-axis represents the correction, ΔX, ΔY, and ΔZ. In other words, the larger the tristimulus value differences, the larger the correction.

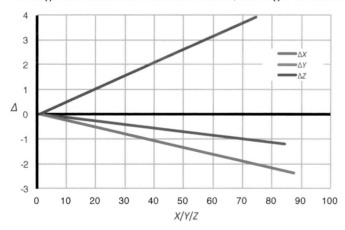

Figure 9.1.

Tristimulus linear correction model.

The SCCA calculation has also been developed in software like PatchTool (Figure 9.2), Curve4, SpotOn, and so on. These software tools are designed to be functional and easy to use.

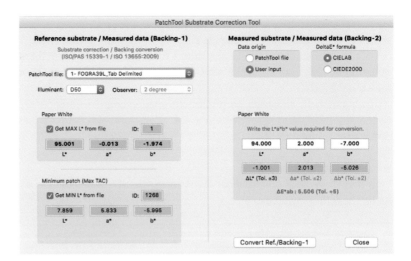

Figure 9.2.
An example of a SCCA calculator

9.9. SCCA Case Study 1: Print to Substrate-corrected Colorimetric Aims

The author of this volume examined the effect of substrate correction on printing conformity (Chung, 2011). The data set aim was Fogra39 with a white point of (95 L^*/0 a^*/−2 b^*). The new substrate, Sappi McCoy, had a white point of (94 L^*/2 a^*/−7 b^*). In this case, the higher negative b^* value is due to the presence of an OBA.

A 20″ × 24″ ink starvation target (Figure 9.3), consisting of color control bars and large right triangle-shaped ink pick-up zones varying from side to side, was printed. By feeding the same ink amount across the width of the ink zones, many solid ink densities can be collected from the color control bar in a single print.

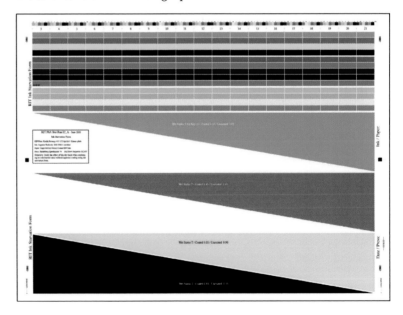

Figure 9.3.
Ink starvation target. (Image courtesy of RIT Printing Applications Laboratory.)

When the minimum ΔE^*_{ab} between measurements and published aims is selected, large color differences in substrates (5.5 ΔE^*_{ab}) and in cyan coloration (3.9 ΔE^*_{ab}) occur before the substrate correction (Table 9.2).

Table 9.2. Color differences before the substrate correction.

	ISO 12647-2 (PT1)					ΔE*$_{ab}$
	L*	a*	b*	C*	h	Inking_1
Paper	95	0	-2	2	270	5.5
	94.1	2.1	-7.0	7	286	
K	16	0	0	0	0	0.7
	16.3	0.4	-0.5	1	311	
C	55	-37	-50	62	233	3.9
	56.4	-33.8	-51.8	62	237	
M	48	74	-3	74	358	0.3
	48.3	74.0	-2.9	74	358	
Y	89	-5	93	93	93	1.5
	88.6	-3.6	92.7	93	92	

Table 9.3 shows that substrate color was reconciled (from 5.5 ΔE^*_{ab} to 0 ΔE^*_{ab}), and the cyan color difference was reduced from 3.9 ΔE^*_{ab} to 2.1 ΔE^*_{ab}.

Table 9.3. Color differences after the substrate correction.

	ISO 12647-2 (PT 1) Corrected					ΔE*$_{ab}$
	L*	a*	b*	C*	h	Inking_2
Paper	94	2	-7	7	286	0.0
	94.1	2.1	-7.0	7	286	
K	16	0	-1	1	292	0.2
	15.8	0.4	-0.5	1	304	
C	54	-36	-54	65	237	2.1
	54.0	-33.6	-53.6	63	238	
M	48	75	-6	75	356	2.5
	49.2	73.3	-4.8	73	356	
Y	88	-3	90	90	92	1.3
	88.8	-4.0	90.6	91	93	

For printing on OBA-loaded papers, (1) SCCA corrects substrate difference completely; (2) low total area coverage (TAC) or highlight areas, having large areas of unprinted paper and high tristimulus values, are corrected proportionally; and (3) high TAC or shadow areas, having low tristimulus values, are corrected less; (4) chromatic colors that do not absorb short-wavelength energies (e.g., cyan and magenta) are affected with respect to their hues: the cyan coloration is improved due to the combination of substrate-corrected aims and correct inking (Figure 9.4), but the magenta solid conformity did not improve; and (5) yellow solid ink, which absorbs short-wavelength energies, has a reduced chroma. In summary, SCCA is not a complete remedy, but it is a first-order correction of OBA-induced color difference.

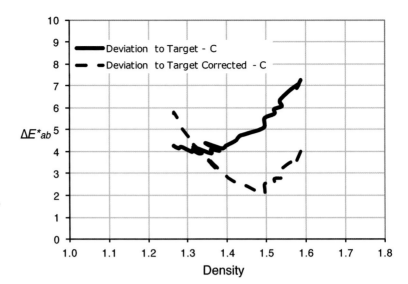

Figure 9.4.
Cyan coloration is improved due to SCCA and correct inking.

9.10. SCCA Case Study 2: Proofing and Printing to Substrate-corrected Colorimetric Aims

This case study sought to determine what it takes to conform to a substrate-corrected data set and the proof–print color match per ISO/PAS 15339-1 (Chung, 2013a). The press was a Goss Sunday 2000 web offset press. The paper was Sappi Opus (white point of 91.4 L^*/0.6 a^*/−6.0 b^*). Two calibration methods were compared: (1) G7 curved plates using Curve2 s/w, and (2) G7+Device-link using Alwan LinkProfiler s/w. Printing and proofing conformance were based on the substrate-corrected SWOP3 (M1) data set and CGATS TR 016 tolerance scheme (CGATS, 2012).

The results showed that G7 calibration missed Level B conformance (Figure 9.5, left); and (G7 + Device-link) calibration achieved Level A conformance (Figure 9.5, right).

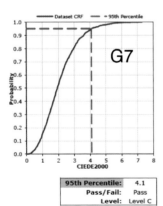

Tagret description	Tolerance (CIEDE2000)		
	Level A	Level B	Level C
95th percentile of all patches of ISO 12642-2	3.0	4.0	5.0
Solid 100C 100M 100Y	1.5	2.4	4.0
100K	2.4	3.6	6.0
50% input tint 50C 50M 50Y 50K	1.5	2.0	2.5
Near-neutral 50C/40M /40Y	3.0	3.5	5.0

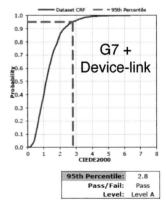

95th Percentile:	4.1
Pass/Fail:	Pass
Level:	Level C

95th Percentile:	2.8
Pass/Fail:	Pass
Level:	Level A

Figure 9.5.
G7 calibration result (left) and G7 + Device-link calibration result (right).

The lesson learned was that achieving data set conformance using OBA paper requires both SCCA and an effective press calibration technique. In this case, the device-link calibration is more capable of reconciling color differences between the substrate-corrected SWOP3 data set aims and the actual printing condition than the G7 method alone.

The proof–print color match was assessed in an ISO 3664–compliant viewing booth (ISO, 2009a). A simulation of the proof-print color match is shown in Figure 9.6. The OBA print (center) conforms to ISO/

PAS 15339-1 using (G7+Device-link) calibration. The SWOP3 proof (left) shows yellowness in the paper and highlight in comparison to the bluish-white of the OBA print (center); and the SCCA proof (right), conforming to ISO/PAS 15339-1 using the device-link profile, match the print (center) closely.

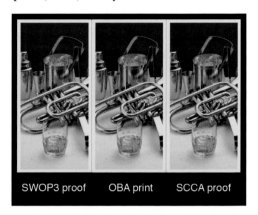

Figure 9.6.
Proof–print color match (simulated).

This case study demonstrates that proofing and printing to the same substrate-corrected data set (M1) provides proof–print color match in the ISO 3664 (ISO, 2009a) viewing conditions.

9.11.   SCCA Case Study 3: The Effect of SCCA on Data Set Conformity

A case study investigated the effect of substrate correction on data set conformity based on 60 (offset, digital printing, and proofing) jobs (Chung and Wu, 2014). Two research questions were identified. The first question was, How many jobs whose paper color conform to ISO 12647-2 (Grade 1) paper specifications? The second question was, What is the effect of substrate correction on data set conformity for these jobs, according to CGATS TR 016 (CGATS, 2012)? The results show that 33 out of 60 (55%) jobs whose substrates conform to ISO 12647-2 (Grade 1) paper specifications; and the other 27 (45%) jobs are out of specifications as these papers are all bluer due to OBA presence (Figure 9.7).

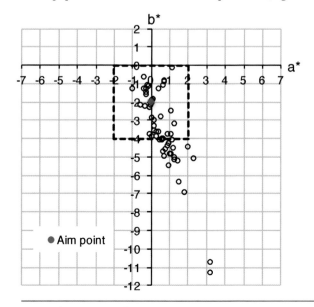

Figure 9.7.
Conformity of paper color according to ISO 12647-2 tolerance.

To answer the second question, Figure 9.8 shows that substrate correction alone, that is, without inking adjustments, benefits color conformity regardless of the substrate type. In other words, when the color difference between the substrate aim point and the actual paper is removed, data set conformity improves in conformity level with less conformity failure.

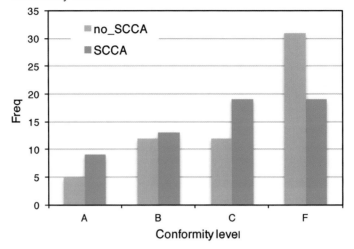

Figure 9.8.
Effect of SCCA on color conformity of 60 jobs.

This case study supports the importance of SCCA when print buyers demand OBA-loaded papers and proof-to-print color match. When implementing SCCA in the printing and proofing workflows, (1) printing-process control metrics (e.g., solids, TVI, MTS) must be derived from the substrate-corrected CRPC, and (2) the substrate-corrected ICC profile must be used as the source in the construction of the device-link profile for color proofing.

9.12.   CGATS TR 016: Tolerance and Conformity Assessment

A characterization data set specifies a printing (or calibration) aim. But there is no published tolerance associated with data set conformity. Existing test methods (e.g., ISO 12647-2 [ISO, 2013b]) are based on limited patches, and the tolerance scheme takes a one-size-fits-all approach. Thus there is a need for a test method to address printing conformity to a data set with a multilevel tolerance scheme. These are the motivations behind the development of CGATS TR 016, *Graphic Technology—Printing Tolerance and Conformity Assessment*.

CGATS TR 016 was first published in January 2012. It was revised in 2014. The test method in CGATS TR 016 (CGATS, 2014) specifies colorimetric measurements according to ISO 13655 (ISO, 2009b), that is, it requires an M1 measurement condition, white backing associated with the reference color characterization data. It also requires substrate correction to be applied to a specified CRPC, and process control aims for printing-process control.

CGATS TR 016 specifies calibration tolerances ranging from relaxed to stringent tolerances. The tolerance scheme is positioned to harmonize the tolerance settings by providing a single reference that could be used to support many printing standards and conformity assessment documents (e.g., ISO 19302 [2017b], Idealliance G7 Colorspace [2018]).

The inaugural edition of CGATS TR 016 specifies three levels (A, B, C) of calibration conformity in terms of ΔE_{00}, ranging from 3.0 to 4.0 to 5.0 (CGATS, 2012). Its revision extends the tolerance to 4 levels (I, II, III, IV), as shown in Table 9.4, to accommodate a wider range of printing processes and applications (CGATS, 2014).

Table 9.4. CGATS TR 016 (2014) tolerance schema.

Control patch description	Level I	Level II	Level III	Level IV
All patches of the ISO 12642-2				
C, M, Y, K solids	$2.0\,\Delta E_{00}$	$3.0\,\Delta E_{00}$	$4.5\,\Delta E_{00}$	$6.0\,\Delta E_{00}$
C, M, Y, K midtone tints				
C50M40Y40 tint				

To explain, tolerances for calibration deviation are specified in terms of the 95th percentile ΔE_{00}. Level I (2.0 ΔE_{00}) tolerance may apply to brand color reproduction using specially formulated inks; level II (3.0 ΔE_{00}) tolerance may apply to contract proofs and brand color reproduction using process inks; level III (4.5 ΔE_{00}) tolerance may apply to commercial printing using coated stock; and level IV (6.0 ΔE_{00}) tolerance may apply to less critical color image reproduction. As the tolerance becomes more stringent, the cost of producing the job should match.

Future revision of CGATS TR 016 should consider the distinction between calibration conformity and production conformity. It should separate between production deviation and production variation. This means that:

1. "Tolerance for deviation," should be labeled "Tolerance for calibration deviation." Calibration deviation is the color difference (95th percentile ΔE_{00}) between color measurements of limited color characterization targets (two or three samples), plus other color patches, and their aim points.
2. "Tolerance for production variation," should be labeled "Tolerance for production deviation and production variation," that is, (a) production deviation is the color difference (70th percentile ΔE_{00}) between the production center of limited patches from a color-control bar (15–20 samples) and the aim point; and (b) production variation is the color difference (70th percentile ΔE_{00}) between the production center of limited patches from a color-control bar (15–20 samples) and each sample.

9.13. Revision of ISO 3664: Viewing Conditions

Color vision, varying from individual to individual, cannot be standardized. But the color viewing condition can be standardized. Outdoor daylight is ideal for viewing color, but daylight changes from dawn to dusk and is not always available. Standardizing color viewing stations for color appraisal becomes an important issue.

As technologies change and print buyers' needs increase, revising existing standards is as important as creating new standards. ISO 3664, *Graphic Technology and Photography—Viewing Conditions* (ISO, 2009a) replaces its previous edition (ISO 3664: 2000) to address color viewing needs.

ISO 3664 specifies five requirements that enable lighting manufacturers to design and manufacture color viewing devices. The five normative requirements are

1. Spectral power distribution of the light source: D50.

2. Intensity of the light source: 2000 lux for critical appraisal and 500 lux for practical appraisal.

3. Evenness of lighting intensity: within 60% between center and corner of the viewing area.

4. Viewing surround: neutral and matte.

5. Viewing geometry: light source, image, and observer positioned such that glare is minimized.

Figure 9.9 is an ISO 3664-compliant viewing station, courtesy of gti, Inc. Other than complying to ISO 3664 requirements, viewing station suppliers face many engineering challenges, including lamp accuracy, lamp life usage, and ergonomics, among others.

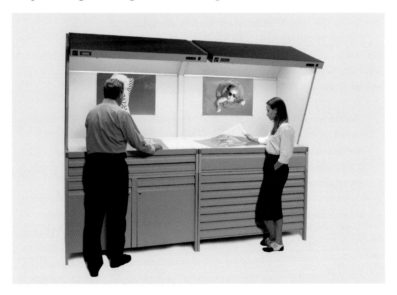

Figure 9.9.
An example of an ISO-compliant viewing station. (Image courtesy of gti, Inc.)

ISO 3664 does not specify how to view and compare two or more color images. Yet there are two viewing conditions that can influence the outcome of visual observation: (1) sequential viewing and (2) simultaneous viewing.

Sequential viewing means viewing one object at a time. Sequential viewing allows the eye to adapt to the white point of the stimulus, thus negating the white point difference between two objects. Viewing color on a monitor in deemed lighting and inspecting a print in a viewing booth are examples of sequential viewing.

Simultaneous viewing means viewing both objects side by side. Simultaneous viewing allows the eye to compare the difference between the two images, including their white points. For example, designers and print buyers often compare the print and the color proof at the same time.

When two colors are viewed simultaneously under the ISO 3664-compliant viewing conditions and matched visually, there is no guarantee that the two colors (e.g., a specially formulated ink and a CMYK-build) will match in other lighting conditions, for examples, daylight (D65), fluorescent (F2, F11), LED, etc. The use of the index of metamerism, discussed in section 2.19, to predict color mismatch with other illuminants may be of value for color-critical customers.

9.14.   Revision of ISO 13655: Color-Measurement Conditions

Substrates containing OBAs are common in papermaking. Printed color containing OBA changes when viewed under different lighting conditions. Light sources used in legacy (existing) color-measurement instruments are unable to detect the OBA presence accurately, thus resulting in variations in color measurement.

ISO 13655, *Graphic Technology—Spectral Measurement and Colorimetric Computation for Graphic Arts Images* (ISO, 2009b), specifies four distinct measurement illumination conditions to enable instrument manufacturers to design and manufacture color-measurement devices (Cheydleur and O'Connor, 2011).

1. Measurement condition M0 represents Illuminant A, used by existing spectrophotometers and densitometers. UV content of the light source in the instrument is not defined. M0 is applicable to measurement conditions where no OBA is present either in substrate or colorant. In other words, M0 is not recommended for use when measuring a press sheet containing OBA.

2. Measurement condition M1 is intended to reduce variations in color measurement between spectrophotometers due to OBA presence. It specifies the spectral power distribution of the light source according to D50. M1 is applicable to measurement conditions where OBA is present in the substrate and colorant.

3. Measurement condition M2 defines the UV exclusion (also known as UV-cut or no UV) condition. M2 is useful where there is a desire to eliminate the fluorescence effect from affecting color data. In addition, the $b*$ difference between M1 measurement and M2 measurement is an indication of the amount of OBA in a substrate.

4. Measurement condition M3 defines the effect of polarization. M3 is used in a measuring instrument to minimize the first surface reflection. Thus it eliminates the difference between wet ink film and dry ink film readings.

Print purchasing trends indicate that print buyers demand OBA-loaded papers and print-to-number. The M1 measurement condition is becoming a default in the printing industry.

9.15.   Future Revision of ISO 12647-2: Offset Lithographic Processes

ISO/IEC 17067 (2013c) specifies three aspects of product conformity. To align with the conformity standard, the printing standard, for example,

ISO 12647-2, should consider the revision of (1) calibration deviation as the color difference between initial (OK) sheets (two or three samples) and the aim points; (2) production deviation as the color difference between production center (15–20 samples) and the aim points; and (3) production variation as the color difference between sample measurements (15–20 samples) and the production center, not the OK print.

9.16. Managing Change

The printing business is about managing print buyers' changing needs. When print buyers prefer color reproduction over monochrome reproduction, printers have to invest in multi-color press acquisition. When print buyers no longer do on-site press checking, but demand printing and proofing to specifications, printers have to invest in dedicated proofing systems and purchase color-measurement instruments. When print buyers prefer to do business with certified print suppliers, printers have to purchase printing-process control software, provide process control training to their press operators, and seek printing certification.

When print buyers demand OBA-loaded (whiter and brighter) paper, and, at the same time, print to numbers, standardization bodies have to revise the lighting and color-measurement standards, and develop a method for printing and proofing to actual printing conditions. Printers have to update their color workflow software and hardware, including color viewing booth and spectrophotometer, accordingly.

Printing business managers must recognize their print buyers' changing needs; give employees the tools, including training, to meet those changing needs; and decide how best to integrate the tools in the workflow. In addition, printing business managers must recognize that the speed of change in production workflows and software upgrades must keep pace with their print buyers' changing needs.

9.17. Chapter Summary

To meet print buyers' needs, the printing industry and printing standardization bodies have been embracing significant changes. New standards (e.g., ISO 15311 and ISO 15339) are developed, and existing standards (e.g., ISO 3664 and ISO 13655) are revised to enable more efficient color imaging workflows.

There is discrepancy in how sampling, deviation, and variation are specified between the ISO/TC 130 community and the ISO/CASCO conformity assessment community. It is recommended that printing standards be revised as follows:

1. Define calibration deviation as the color difference between initial press sheets (two or three samples) and the aim points.

2. Define production deviation as the color difference between the production center (15–20 samples) and the aim points. When the production center is not aligned to the aim, job-to-job color consistency may be in jeopardy. Production deviation can be corrected by process recalibration.

3. Define production variation as the color difference between the production center and sample measurements (15–20 samples). When

the production variation is too large, within-job color consistency is in jeopardy. Root causes of the variation must be discovered and fixed before recalibration.

9.18. Multiple-Choice and Essay Questions

1. Print buyers have the right to _____.
A. specify printing requirements
B. receive quality printed products
C. be informed of the supplier's quality
D. All of the above

2. _____ integrates text, vector graphics, and images in a single document.
A. DDES (Digital Data Exchange Standard)
B. CGATS TR 001
C. PDF/X
D. SCCA

3. _____ assumes that the printing aim is a reference characterization data set.
A. ISO 12647-2
B. ISO 13655
C. ISO 3664
D. ISO/TS 15311-1

4. Achieving data set conformance using OBA paper requires _____.
A. SCCA
B. effective press calibration technique
C. Both A and B
D. None of the above

5. After press proofs, _____ proofs became viable alternatives from 1980 to 2000.
A. photo-mechanical
B. silver halide
C. electro-photographic
D. inkjet

6. ISO/PAS 15339-1 reconciles the "proof-and-print mismatch" problem due to the presence of OBA by _____.
A. using the M0 measurement condition
B. revising the tolerances of printing specification
C. introducing SCCA
D. None of the above

7. CGATS TR 016 defines calibration deviation as the difference between _____.
A. the measurement of the initial sheet and the aim points
B. the measurement of the initial sheet and the sample measurements
C. the production average and sample measurements
D. the production average and the aim points

8. _____ is the common metric that specifies color tolerances in CGATS TR 016.

A. ΔE_{00}

B. ΔE^*_{ab}

C. ΔC_h

D. ΔH

9. Inkjet or digital color proofs rely on _____ to provide appearance match to the press sheet.

A. tight media control

B. device calibration

C. color-management systems

D. All of the above

10. The _____ difference between M1 measurement and M2 measurement is an indication of the amount of OBA in substrate.

A. a^*

B. b^*

C. L^*

D. ΔC^*

11. Why is it strategic to separate "production deviation" from "production variation" in printing-process control?

12. In what way has the relationship between proofing and printing changed in the past 40 years?

Appendix A.
List of Figures and Tables

Appendix B.
List of Equations

Chapter 1. Densitometry

Reflection density and reflectance

$$D_R = \log_{10} \frac{1}{R}$$ Eq. 1.1

$$R = 10^{-D_R}$$ Eq. 1.2

Transmission density and film dot area (FDA)

$$D_T = \log_{10} \frac{1}{T}$$ Eq. 1.3

$$T = 10^{-D_T}$$ Eq. 1.4

$$\%FDA = (1 - T) \times 100$$ Eq. 1.5
$$= (1 - 10^{-D_T}) \times 100$$

$$D_T = \log_{10} \frac{1}{\left[\frac{100-\%FDA}{100}\right]}$$ Eq. 1.6

$$\Delta D_T = \log_{10} \frac{1}{\left[\frac{100-10}{100}\right]} - \log_{10} \frac{1}{\left[\frac{100-5}{100}\right]} = 0.05 - 0.02 = 0.03$$ Eq. 1.7

$$\Delta D_T = \log_{10} \frac{1}{\left[\frac{100-95}{100}\right]} - \log_{10} \frac{1}{\left[\frac{100-90}{100}\right]} = 1.30 - 1.00 = 0.30$$ Eq. 1.8

TVI (Murray-Davies equation)

$$\%TVI = \% \, Dot_{Print} - \% \, Dot_{Film \, (Digital)}$$ Eq. 1.9

$$\% \, Dot_{Print} = \frac{1 - 10^{-(Dt-Dp)}}{1 - 10^{-(Ds-Dp)}} \times 100$$ Eq. 1.10

$$\% \, Dot_{Film} = \left[1 - 10^{-(Dt-Dp)}\right] \times 100$$ Eq. 1.11

Print contract

$$\%PC = \left[\frac{Ds-D75}{Ds}\right] \times 100$$ Eq. 1.12

Apparent ink trap

$$\% \, Apparent \, ink \, trap = \frac{D3-D1}{D2} \times 100$$ Eq. 1.13

Midtone spread (MTS)

$$\text{MTS} = \text{Max}\left[(A_c - A_{co}), (A_m - A_{mo}), (A_y - A_{yo})\right] - \text{Min}\left[(A_c - A_{co}), (A_m - A_{mo}), (A_y - A_{yo})\right] \qquad \text{Eq. 1.14}$$

A_x is measured tonal value,

A_{xo} is specified aim points,

Where x is c, m, and y

Hue error, efficiency, and grayness

$$\% \text{ Hue error} = \left(\frac{D_M - D_L}{D_H - D_L}\right) \times 100 \qquad \text{Eq. 1.15}$$

$$\% \text{ Efficiency} = \left(1 - \frac{D_M + D_L}{2 \times D_H}\right) \times 100 \qquad \text{Eq. 1.16}$$

$$\% \text{ Grayness} = \frac{D_L}{D_H} \times 100 \qquad \text{Eq. 1.17}$$

Chapter 2. Colorimetry

Tristimulus integration (spectral-to-color)

$$X = k \sum_{400}^{700} P_{(\lambda)} R_{(\lambda)}\, x_{(\lambda)} \qquad \text{Eq. 2.1}$$

$$Y = k \sum_{400}^{700} P_{(\lambda)} R_{(\lambda)}\, y_{(\lambda)} \qquad \text{Eq. 2.2}$$

$$Z = k \sum_{400}^{700} P_{(\lambda)} R_{(\lambda)}\, z_{(\lambda)} \qquad \text{Eq. 2.3}$$

$$k = \frac{100}{\sum P_{(\lambda)}\, y_{(\lambda)}} \qquad \text{Eq. 2.4}$$

$$X = \sum_{400}^{700} R(\lambda) \times W_X(\lambda) \qquad \text{Eq. 2.5}$$

$$Y = \sum_{400}^{700} R(\lambda) \times W_Y(\lambda) \qquad \text{Eq. 2.6}$$

$$Z = \sum_{400}^{700} R(\lambda) \times W_Z(\lambda) \qquad \text{Eq. 2.7}$$

$R(\lambda)$ is the reflectance factor at λ.

$W_x(\lambda)$ is the weighting factor at λ for tristimulus value X.

$W_y(\lambda)$ is the weighting factor at λ for tristimulus value Y.

$W_z(\lambda)$ is the weighting factor at λ for tristimulus value Z.

Chromaticity (x, y)

$$x = \frac{X}{X + Y + Z} \qquad \text{Eq. 2.8}$$

$$y = \frac{Y}{X + Y + Z} \qquad \text{Eq. 2.9}$$

Calculating CIELAB from XYZ

$$L* = 116\left[f\left(\frac{Y}{Y_n}\right)\right] - 16 \qquad \text{Eq. 2.10}$$

$$a* = 500\left[f\left(\frac{X}{X_n}\right) - f\left(\frac{Y}{Y_n}\right)\right] \qquad \text{Eq. 2.11}$$

$$b* = 200\left[f\left(\frac{Y}{Y_n}\right) - f\left(\frac{Z}{Z_n}\right)\right] \qquad \text{Eq. 2.12}$$

X, Y, and Z are the tristimulus values.

X_n, Y_n, and Z_n are the white point.

Metric chroma (C^*) and chroma difference (ΔC^*)

$$C* = \sqrt{a*^2 + b*^2} \qquad\qquad \text{Eq. 2.13}$$

$$\Delta C^* = C_1{}^* - C_2{}^* \qquad\qquad \text{Eq. 2.14}$$

Hue angle (h)

$$h_{\text{Radian}} = \tan^{-1}\left(\frac{b*}{a*}\right) \qquad\qquad \text{Eq. 2.15}$$

$$h_{\text{Degree}} = h_{\text{Radian}} \times \frac{180}{\pi} \qquad\qquad \text{Eq. 2.16}$$

Chromaticness difference (ΔC_h)

$$\Delta C_h = \sqrt{\Delta a*^2 + \Delta b*^2} \qquad\qquad \text{Eq. 2.17}$$

$$\Delta a* = a*_1 - a*_2 \qquad\qquad \text{Eq. 2.18}$$

$$\Delta b* = b*_1 - b*_2 \qquad\qquad \text{Eq. 2.19}$$

XYZ-derived TVI

$$\text{TVI}_{M\&K} = 100\left[\frac{Y_p - Y_t}{Y_p - Y_s}\right] - \text{TV}_{\text{Input}} \qquad\qquad \text{Eq. 2.20}$$

$$\text{TVI}_Y = 100\left[\frac{Z_p - Z_t}{Z_p - Z_s}\right] - \text{TV}_{\text{Input}} \qquad\qquad \text{Eq. 2.21}$$

$$\text{TVI}_C = 100\left[\frac{(X_p - 0.55Z_p) - (X_t - 0.55Z_t)}{(X_p - 0.55Z_p) - (X_s - 0.55Z_s)}\right] - \text{TV}_{\text{Input}} \qquad \text{Eq. 2.22}$$

Where subscripts: p = paper, t = tint, and s = solid.

Color difference (ΔE^*_{ab})

$$\Delta E*_{ab} = \sqrt{(L*_1 - L*_2)^2 + (a*_1 - a*_2)^2 + (b*_1 - b*_2)^2} \quad \text{Eq. 2.23}$$

Where C_1: L^*_1, a^*_1, b^*_1 and C_2: L^*_2, a^*_2, b^*_2

Hue difference (ΔH^*)

$$\Delta H* = \sqrt{\Delta E*_{ab}{}^2 - \Delta L*^2 - \Delta C*^2} \qquad\qquad \text{Eq. 2.24}$$

$$\Delta h = |h_1 - h_2| \qquad\qquad \text{Eq. 2.25}$$

Mean difference from the mean (MCDM)

$$\text{MCDM} = \frac{\sum_{i=1}^{n} \Delta E(\text{Lab}_{\text{Ave}} - \text{Lab}_i)}{n} \qquad\qquad \text{Eq. 2.26}$$

Chapter 4. Printing Standardization

Spot color tonal value (SCTV)

$$\text{SCTV} = 100 \times \sqrt{\frac{(V_{xt} - V_{xp})^2 + (V_{yt} - V_{yp})^2 + (V_{zt} - V_{zp})^2}{(V_{xs} - V_{xp})^2 + (V_{ys} - V_{yp})^2 + (V_{zs} - V_{zp})^2}} \qquad \text{Eq. 4.1}$$

where V_{xs}, V_{ys}, and V_{zs} are values of the spot color solid,
V_{xp}, V_{yp}, and V_{zp} are values of the substrate, and
V_{xt}, V_{yt}, and V_{zt} are values of the spot color tint.

Chapter 6. Device Calibration

Tollenaar equation

$$D = \text{SD}(1 - e^{-mw})$$

Eq. 6.1

D is the solid ink density of the print.

SD (saturation density) is the density of an infinitely thick ink film.

m is the rate at which the SD is approached.

w is the ink film thickness.

Near-neutral triplets

$$M = Y = 0.747C - 4.1{\times}10^{-4}C^2 + 2.94{\times}10^{-5}C^3$$

Eq. 6.2

Gray reproduction curves (a^* and b^* as a function of TV_C)

$$a^*(\text{TV}_C) = a^*{}_S \times \left(1 - \frac{\text{TV}_C}{100}\right)$$

Eq. 6.3

$$b^*(\text{TV}_C) = b^*{}_S \times \left(1 - \frac{\text{TV}_C}{100}\right)$$

Eq. 6.4

Chapter 7. Printing-Process Control

Beer's law

$$R_\lambda = 10^{-\{[(D_\lambda - D_p)\cdot t] + D_p\}}$$

Eq. 7.1

$$R_\lambda = R_p \cdot \left[\frac{R_s}{R_p}\right]^t$$

Eq. 7.2

Derivation from Eq. 7.2 to Eq. 7.1

$$R_\lambda = R_p \cdot \left(\frac{R_s}{R_p}\right)^t$$

$$= 10^{-D_p} \cdot \left(\frac{10^{-D_s}}{10^{-D_p}}\right)^t$$

$$= 10^{-D_p} \cdot \left(10^{-D_s + D_p}\right)^t$$

$$= 10^{-D_p} \cdot \left(10^{D_p - D_s}\right)^t$$

$$= 10^{-D_p} \cdot 10^{(D_p - D_s)t}$$

$$= 10^{(D_p - D_s)t - D_p}$$

$$= 10^{-[(D_s - D_p)t + D_p]}$$

Sample average (X_bar)

$$X\_bar = \frac{\sum_{i=1}^{n} X_i}{n}$$

Eq. 7.3

Sample standard deviation (s)

Eq. 7.4

$$s = \sqrt{\frac{\sum_{i=1}^{n} (X_i - X\_bar)^2}{n-1}}$$

Process capability, CP and CpK

$$CP = \frac{\text{Tolerance}}{6\sigma} = \frac{\text{USL}-\text{LSL}}{6s}$$

Eq. 7.5

$$CpK = \text{The lesser of } \frac{(\text{USL}-\text{mean})}{3\sigma}$$

Eq. 7.6

$$\text{or } \frac{(\text{mean} - \text{LSL})}{3\sigma}$$

Chapter 9. Printing Standards in a Changing Industry

SCCA

$$X_2 = X_1(1 + C) - X_{\min}C$$

Eq. 9.1

$$C = \frac{X_{w2}-X_{w1}}{X_{w1}-X_{\min}}$$

Eq. 9.2

X_1 is the tristimulus value of printed color on Substrate_1.

X_2 is the corrected tristimulus value of printed color on Substrate_2.

C is a constant (slope).

X_{w1} is the measured tristimulus value of Substrate_1.

X_{w2} is the measured tristimulus value of Substrate_2.

$X_{\min}$ is the minimum tristimulus value of Substrate_1

(The quantity, $X_{\min}$, may be substituted by $10L^*$, $0a^*$, $0b^*$ for coated paper).

Appendix C.
Answers to Multiple-Choice and Essay Questions

Chapter 1. Densitometry
Multiple-Choice questions

1.1	1.2	1.3	1.4	1.5	1.6	1.7	1.8	1.9	1.10
A	C	B	D	C	D	B	A	B	B

Essay questions

1.11   Controlling solid coloration is an important step in printing-process control. A densitometer can quantify and differentiate dark shades better than the human eye.

1.12   TVI is the darkening of the halftone tints as the film dots or digital dots are transferred to paper. The darkening is caused by the spread of the printed dots at the printing nip (physical dot gain). The darkening is also caused by light penetrating unprinted paper, being trapped by printed dots, and never exiting from the paper (optical dot gain).

Chapter 2. Colorimetry
Multiple-Choice questions

2.1	2.2	2.3	2.4	2.5	2.6	2.7	2.8	2.9	2.10
B	C	C	A	A	C	D	A	C	B

Essay questions

2.11   Metamerism is the fundamental principle that serves as the basis for color matching. It is a blessing, because the match will result when the measurement, the illumination, and the observer are accounted for. It is also a curse, because the match no longer holds if the measurement, the illumination, or the observer is changed.

2.12 ΔC^* is the chroma difference between two colors, or $\Delta C^* = C_1^* - C_2^*$. ΔC_h (Chromaticness difference) is the difference between the reference chroma (a^*_1 and b^*_1) and the measured chroma (a^*_2 and b^*_2) of a neutral patch, e.g., C50 M40Y40, or $\Delta C_h = \sqrt{\Delta a *^2 + \Delta b *^2}$.

Chapter 3. The ICC Color-Management System

Multiple-Choice questions

3.1	3.2	3.3	3.4	3.5	3.6	3.7	3.8	3.9	3.10
A	C	C	A	B	A	A	B	A	B

Essay questions

3.11   A CMYK printer profile describes the color behavior of the printer at a given ink-paper-printing condition between its CMYK values and the CIELAB values. The CMYK printer profile only works for the printer at its calibrated state, and not at altered states. Thus, a CMYK printer profile is device dependent.

3.12   *Assign Profile* changes the definition of the color data and the appearance of the image (if different from the working space). The value of the color data in the image is not altered.

Chapter 4. Printing Standardization

Multiple-Choice questions

4.1	4.2	4.3	4.4	4.5	4.6	4.7	4.8	4.9	4.10
A	A	B	A	D	C	A	A	B	B

Essay questions

4.11   *Shall* is normative, and it means "must comply" to a more relaxed tolerance; *should* is informative and it means "nice to comply" to a more stringent tolerance. For example, spot color tolerance shall be 3.0 ΔE_{00} and should be 2.0 ΔE_{00}.

4.12   ISO 12647-2 uses measurements of solids, TVIs, and MTS from multiple samples and the OK sheet for production variation assessment. The conformity is based on 68% conformity ("7 out of 10" rule).

Chapter 5. Printing Conformity Assessment

Multiple-Choice questions

5.1	5.2	5.3	5.4	5.5	5.6	5.7	5.8	5.9	5.10
D	B	A	B	C	D	B	A	C	B

Essay questions

5.11   There are printing process-dependent standards that specify process control parameters as printing aims, e.g., ISO 12647-2 for offset printing, ISO 12647-4 for gravure printing, and ISO 12647-6 for flexographic printing requirements.

       There is also a printing process-independent standard, i.e., ISO 15339-1, that specifies a characterization data set as printing aims.

5.12   This is because the needs of print buyers and brand owners to manage the complex supply chains are the greatest motivation for printers to get certified.

Chapter 6. Device Calibration

Multiple-Choice questions

6.1	6.2	6.3	6.4	6.5	6.6	6.7	6.8	6.9	6.10
B	B	D	A	A	B	A	D	C	A

Essay questions

6.11   Device calibration in process color printing is the adjustment of a printing device to specified aim values. This can be accomplished by physical means, e.g., ink film thickness change, or by altering digital input values.

6.12   In general, solid ink density (SID) is proportional to ink film thickness (IFT). But, SID cannot be increased indefinitely due to the saturation density limit, per the Tollenaar equation.

Chapter 7. Printing-Process Control

Multiple-Choice questions

7.1	7.2	7.3	7.4	7.5	7.6	7.7	7.8	7.9	7.10
B	C	C	C	A	D	D	B	C	C

Essay questions

7.11   The first step is to adjust image-to-image registration and ink film thickness during press makeready. The second step is to calibrate the process to achieve deviation conformity. The third step is to implement process control to achieve production variation conformity.

7.12   Beer's law states that when light passes through a liquid, the light absorption is proportional to the concentration and the path length of the liquid. Beer's law provides a mathematic model regarding changes in solid ink density that best matches the specified CIELAB values.

Chapter 8. *Test Targets*: A Teaching and Learning Journey

Multiple-Choice questions

8.1	8.2	8.3	8.4	8.5	8.6	8.7	8.8	8.9	8.10
B	B	B	B	D	D	C	A	C	D

Essay questions

8.11   Cyan, magenta, or yellow ink, each absorbing one-third of the spectrum, produces a large color gamut. Red, green, or blue ink, each absorbing two-thirds of the spectrum, produces a small gamut (no yellow). Thus, CMY inks are suitable for pictorial color reproduction.

8.12   The eye sees the 150 lpi line screen (or 6 cycles per millimeter) a uniform area rather than separate lines at the normal viewing distance. This is the reason a 150 lpi halftone screen became a de facto standard for commercial printing.

Chapter 9. Printing Standards in a Changing Industry

Multiple-Choice questions

9.1	9.2	9.3	9.4	9.5	9.6	9.7	9.8	9.9	9.10
D	C	D	C	A	C	A	A	D	B

Essay questions

9.11   Production deviation is the difference between the production average and the aim points. When the production average is not aligned to the aim points, it can be corrected by process recalibration. On the other hand, if the production variation is too large, root causes of the variation must be discovered and fixed before process recalibration.

9.12   The relationship between proofing and printing has changed from "print to match a proof" in the past to "proof and print to match a specified color characterization data set" today.

Bibliography

Berns, Roy S. *Billmeyer and Saltzman's Principles of Color Technology.* 3rd ed. New York: Wiley, 2000.

Birch, J., *Diagnosis of Defective Colour Vision.* 2nd ed. Oxford: Butterworth-Heinemann, 2001.

Brunner, Felix. "Brunner Picture Contrast Profile." *TAGA Proceedings* 1987: 256–263.

bvdm. *Roman16 Images.* Berlin, Germany: bvdm, 2013. www.bvdm-online.de/themen/technik-forschung/standardwerke/roman16.

bvdm. *Media Standard Print, Technical Guidelines for Data, Proof and Production Run Printing.* Berlin, Germany: bvdm, 2016. www.bvdm-online.de.

CGATS (Committee for Graphic Arts Technology Standards). *Graphic Technology—Specifications for Graphic Arts Printing—Type 1.* CGATS TR 001. Reston, VA: ANSI, 1995.

CGATS (Committee for Graphic Arts Technology Standards). CGATS TR 016, *Graphic Technology—Printing Tolerance and Conformity Assessment.* Reston, VA: CGATS, ANSI, 2012.

CGATS (Committee for Graphic Arts Technology Standards). CGATS TR 015, *Graphic Technology—Methodology for Establishing Printing Aims Based on a Shared Near-Neutral Gray-Scale.* Reston, VA: ANSI, 2013.

CGATS (Committee for Graphic Arts Technology Standards). CGATS TR 016, *Graphic Technology—Printing Tolerance and Conformity Assessment.* Reston, VA: CGATS, ANSI, 2014. http://www.npes.org/programs/standardsworkroom/toolsbestpractices/technicalreports.aspx

Cheydleur, Raymond, and Kevin O'Connor. *"The M Factor... What Does It Mean?"* Grand Rapids, MI: X-Rite, 2011. https://www.xrite.com/-/media/xrite/files/literature/17/17-500_17-599/17-510_m_factor_what_does_it_mean/17-510_m_factor_en.pdf.

Chung, Robert. "Color Control for Process Color Printing: Eyeball vs. SPC." *TAPPI Symposium Proceedings on Process and Product Quality*, October 29–31, 1991.

Chung, Robert. "Gravure Research Agenda: The Journey of a Test Form from Engraving to Proofing." *Gravure*, February 2006, pp. 42–47.

Chung, Robert. "Substrate Correction in ISO 12647-2." *TAGA Proceedings* 2011: 34–47.

Chung, Robert. "Conformance to Substrate-corrected Dataset, a Case Study." *TAGA Proceedings* 2013: 89–99.

Chung, Robert and Ping-hsu Chen. "Determining CIEDE2000 for Printing Conformance." Pp. 11–18 in *Proceedings of the 38th IARIGAI Research Conference, Advances in Color Reproduction*, Budapest, Hungary, 2011.

Chung, Robert, and Li-Yi Ma. "Press Performance Comparison between AM and FM Screening." *TAGA Proceedings* 1995: 321–328.

Chung, Robert, and Yoshikazu Shimamura. "Quantitative Analysis of Pictorial Color Image Difference." *TAGA Proceedings* 2001: 381–398.

Chung, Robert, and Yi Wang. *Statistical Analyses of the IDEAlliance G7 Master Printer Database*. PICRM-2011-09. Rochester, NY: RIT Printing Industry Center, 2011b. https://scholarworks.rit.edu/cgi/viewcontent.cgi?referer=https://www.google.com/&httpsredir=1&article=1097&context=books.

Chung, Robert, and Li Wu. "The Effect of Substrate Correction on Printing Conformity." *Journal of Print and Media Technology Research* 3, no. 4, 2014: 261–268.

Chung, Robert, Anirban Dutta, Arthur Summerville, Deepak Dubey, Franz Sigg, Ganesh Sivam, Mahadzir Mohamad, and Tanit Viriyarungsarit. *Test Targets 2.0, A Collection of Digital Test Forms Showcasing Features, Capabilities, and Applications in Printing and Publishing*. Rochester, NY: RIT School of Media Sciences, 2002. https://scholarworks.rit.edu/books/68.

Chung, Robert, Franz Sigg, Fred Hsu, Gregory Firestone, Hemachand Kolli, Michael Meyehofer, Nilay Patel, Ryan Testa, Tiago Costa, and Vikaas Gupta. *Test Targets 3.0, A Collection of Digital Test Forms Showcasing Features, Capabilities, and Applications in Printing and Publishing*. Rochester, NY: RIT School of Media Sciences, 2003a. https://scholarworks.rit.edu/books/74.

Chung, Robert, Edline Chun, Fred Hsu, Hemachand Kolli, Jon Lesser, Lingjun Kong, Ryan Testa, Seunga Kang Ha, Somika Shetty, and Vikaas Gupta. *Test Targets 3.1, A Collection of Digital Test Forms Showcasing Features, Capabilities, and Applications in Printing and Publishing.* Rochester, NY: RIT School of Media Sciences, 2003b. https://scholarworks.rit.edu/books/69.

Chung, Robert, Doug Caruso, Edline Chun, Eric Berkow, Franz Sigg, Gregory Zolan, Howard Vogl, Nattawan Techavichien, Rochelle Kim, Tiago Costa, and Wiphut Janjomsuke. *Test Targets 4.0, A Collaborative Effort Exploring the Use of Scientific Methods for Color Imaging and Process Control.* Rochester, NY: RIT School of Media Sciences, 2004. https://scholarworks.rit.edu/books/70.

Chung, Robert, Adam Dewitz, Dimitrios Ploumidis, Edline Chun, Franz Sigg, Fred Hsu, Jorge Uribe, and Michael Riordan. *Test Targets 5.0, A Collaborative Effort Exploring the Use of Scientific Methods for Color Imaging and Process Control.* Rochester, NY: RIT School of Media Sciences, 2005. https://scholarworks.rit.edu/books/73.

Chung, Robert, Franz Sigg, Dimitrios Ploumidis, Henry Freedman, Matthew Rees, Michael Riordan, Fred Hsu, and Doug Caruso. *Test Targets 6.0, A Collaborative Effort Exploring the Use of Scientific Methods for Color Imaging and Process Control.* Rochester, NY: RIT School of Media Sciences, 2006. https://scholarworks.rit.edu/books/75.

Chung, Robert, Arvind Karthikeyan, Franz Sigg, Wuhui Liu, Fred Hsu, and Steve Suffoletto. *Test Targets 7.0, A Collaborative Effort Exploring the Use of Scientific Methods for Color Imaging and Process Control.* Rochester, NY: RIT School of Media Sciences, 2007. https://scholarworks.rit.edu/books/72.

Chung, Robert, Bill Pope, Fred Hsu, Franz Sigg, Evan Andersen, Jiayi Zhou, Khalid Husain, Michael Riordan. *Test Targets 8.0, A Collaborative Effort Exploring the Use of Scientific Methods for Color Imaging and Process Control.* Rochester, NY: RIT School of Media Sciences, 2008. https://scholarworks.rit.edu/books/71.

Chung, Robert, Angelica Li, Anupam Dhopade, Changshi Wu, Fred Hsu, Henry Freedman, and Scott Millward. *Test Targets 9.0.* Rochester, NY: RIT School of Media Sciences, 2009. https://scholarworks.rit.edu/books/103.

Chung, Robert, Elie Khoury, Pierre Urbain, Enqi Zhang, Franz Sigg, Scott Millward, Ivy Tian, and Yi Wang. *Test Targets 10.* Rochester, NY: RIT School of Media Sciences, 2010. https://scholarworks.rit.edu/books/102.

Chung, Robert, Changyong Feng, and Lufei Yu. "Assessing Printing Variation in Terms of Accuracy and Precision." Paper presented at ISO/TC130 Meeting, Shengzhen, China, 2013b.

Chung, Robert, Elena Fedorovskaya, David Hunter, and Pierre Urbain. "Predicting Color Image Match." *TAGA Proceedings* 2017: 132–142.

DataMyte. *DataMyte Handbook, A Practical Guide to Computerized Data Collection for Statistical Process Control.* 4th ed. Minnetonka, MN: DataMyte Corporation, 1989.

Dolezalek, Frederich K. "Appraisal of Production Run Fluctuations from Color Measurements in the Image." *TAGA Proceedings* 1994: 154–165.

Eastman Kodak. Kodak Photographic Filters Handbook, Rochester, NY: 1990.

Elyjiw, Zenon, and H. Brent Archer. "A Practical Approach to Gray Balance and Tone Reproduction in Process Color." *TAGA Proceedings* 1972: 78–97.

Field, Gary. "Ink Trap Measurement." *TAGA Proceedings* 1985: 382–396.

Field, Gary. *Color and Its Reproduction, Fundamental for the Digital Imaging and Printing Industry.* 3rd ed. Pittsburgh, PA: GATF Press, 2004.

FTA (Flexographic Technical Association). *FIRST Company Certification.* Bohemia, NY: FTA, 2019. https://flexography.org/wp-content/uploads/2013/11/FIRSTCompanyCertV3.pdf

Fraser, B., C. Murphy, and Fred Bunting. *Real World Color Management.* 2nd ed. Berkeley, CA: Peachpit Press, 2005.

Hunt, R. W. G. *The Reproduction of Colour in Photography, Printing, and Television.* 4th ed. Tolworth, UK: Fountain Press, 1987.

Idealliance. *G7 Master Pass Fail Requirements.* Version 34. Alexandria, VA: Idealliance, 2018. http://connect.idealliance.org/viewdocument/g7-master-passfail-requirements-1?CommunityKey=637a28 3c-7f9a-4b96-9bdc-7206dc457100&tab=librarydocuments.

Idealliance. *Guide to Print Production.* Version 20.1. Alexandria, VA: Idealliance, 2020. www.idealliance.org.

Ishihara, S. *Test for Color Blindness.* Tokyo: Kanehara Shuppan Co., Ltd., 1962.

ISO (International Organization for Standardization). ISO 12640-1, *Graphic Technology—Prepress Digital Data Exchange—CMYK Standard Color Image Data.* Geneva, Switzerland: ISO, 1995.

ISO (International Organization for Standardization). ISO 13660, *Information Technology—Office Equipment—Measurement of Image Quality Attributes for Hardcopy Output—Binary Monochrome Text and Graphic Images.* Geneva, Switzerland: ISO, 2001.

ISO (International Organization for Standardization). ISO 5-3,
    Photography and Graphic Technology—Density Measurements. Part 3,
    Spectral Conditions. Geneva, Switzerland: ISO, 2002.

ISO (International Organization for Standardization). ISO/TS 19751-1,
    *Office Equipment—Appearance-based Image Quality Standards for
    Printers*. Part 1, *Overview, Procedure and Common Methods*. Geneva,
    Switzerland: ISO, 2004.

ISO (International Organization for Standardization). ISO 12642-2,
    *Graphic Technology—Input Data for Characterization of 4-Colour
    Process Printing*. Part 2, *Expanded Data Set*. Geneva, Switzerland:
    ISO, 2005a.

ISO (International Organization for Standardization). ISO/IEC 17011,
    *Conformity Assessment—General Requirements for Accrediting
    Conformity Assessment Bodies*. Geneva, Switzerland: ISO, 2005b

ISO (International Organization for Standardization). ISO/IEC 17025,
    *General Requirements for the Competence of Testing and Calibration
    Laboratories*. Geneva, Switzerland: ISO, 2005c.

ISO (International Organization for Standardization). ISO/DIS 2846-1,
    *Graphic Technology and Photography— Colour and Transparency of
    Ink Sets for Four-Colour-Printing*. Part 1, *Sheet-fed and Heat-set Web
    Offset Lithographic Printing*. Geneva, Switzerland: ISO, 2006.

ISO (International Organization for Standardization). ISO 12646,
    *Graphic Technology—Displays for Colour Proofing—Characteristics
    and Viewing Conditions*. Geneva, Switzerland: ISO, 2006.

ISO (International Organization for Standardization). ISO 12640-3,
    Graphic Technology—Prepress Digital Data Exchange. Part 3, *CIELAB
    Standard Color Image Data*. Geneva, Switzerland: ISO, 2007a.

ISO (International Organization for Standardization). ISO 15930-7,
    *Graphic Technology—Prepress Digital Data Exchange Using PDF.
    Part 7, Complete Exchange of Printing Data (PDF/X-4) and Partial
    Exchange of Printing Data with External Profile Reference (PDF/X-4p)
    Using PDF 1.6*. Geneva, Switzerland: ISO, 2007b.

ISO (International Organization for Standardization). ISO 9001, *Quality
    Management Systems Requirements*. Geneva, Switzerland: ISO, 2008.

ISO (International Organization for Standardization). ISO 3664,
    Graphic Technology and Photography—Viewing Conditions. Geneva,
    Switzerland: ISO, 2009a.

ISO (International Organization for Standardization). ISO 13655,
    *Graphic Technology—Spectral Measurement and Colorimetric
    Computation for Graphic Arts Images*. Geneva, Switzerland: ISO,
    2009b.

ISO (International Organization for Standardization). ISO/IEC 17007, *Conformity Assessment—Guidance for Drafting Normative Documents Suitable for Use for Conformity Assessment.* Geneva, Switzerland: ISO, 2009c.

ISO (International Organization for Standardization). ISO TC130 N1733 Resolutions of the 24th Plenary Meeting. Sao Paulo, Brazil: ISO, 2010a.

ISO/CASCO (International Organization for Standardization/ Committee on Conformity Assessment). *Building Trust, The Conformity Assessment Toolbox.* Geneva, Switzerland: ISO, 2010b.

ISO (International Organization for Standardization). *ISO/IEC Directives.* Part 1, *Procedures for the Technical Work.* Geneva, Switzerland: ISO, 2011a.

ISO (International Organization for Standardization). ISO/IEC 17021, *Conformity Assessment—Requirements for Bodies Providing Audit and Certification of Management Systems.* Geneva, Switzerland: ISO, 2011b.

ISO (International Organization for Standardization). ISO 17972-4, *Graphic Technology—Colour Data Exchange Format (CxF/X-4).* Part 4, *Spot Colour Characterisation Data.* Geneva, Switzerland: ISO, 2011c.

ISO (International Organization for Standardization). ISO 12647-1, *Graphic Technology—Process Control for the Production of Half-Tone Colour Separations, Proof and Production Prints.* Part 1, *Parameters and Measurement Methods.* Geneva, Switzerland: ISO, 2012a.

ISO (International Organization for Standardization). ISO 12647-6, *Graphic Technology—Process Control for the Manufacture of Half-Tone Colour Separations, Proof and Production Prints.* Part 6, *Flexographic Printing.* Geneva, Switzerland: ISO, 2012b.

ISO (International Organization for Standardization). ISO 12647-8, *Graphic Technology—Validation Print Processes Working Directly from Digital Data.* Geneva, Switzerland: ISO, 2012c.

ISO (International Organization for Standardization). ISO/IEC 17065, *Conformity Assessment—Requirements for Bodies Certifying Products, Processes and Services.* Geneva, Switzerland: ISO, 2012d.

ISO (International Organization for Standardization). ISO 12647-2, *Graphic Technology—Process Control for the Manufacture of Half-Tone Colour Separations, Proof and Production Prints.* Part 2, *Offset Lithographic Processes.* Geneva, Switzerland: ISO, 2013a.

ISO (International Organization for Standardization). ISO 14861, *Graphic Technology—Requirements for Colour Soft Proofing Systems*. Geneva, Switzerland: ISO, 2013b.

ISO (International Organization for Standardization). ISO/IEC 17067, *Conformity Assessment—Fundamentals of Product Certification and Guidelines for Product Certification Schemes*. Geneva, Switzerland: ISO, 2013c.

ISO (International Organization for Standardization). ISO/TS 10128, *Graphic Technology—Methods of Adjustment of the Colour Reproduction of a Printing System to Match a Set of Characterization Data*. Geneva, Switzerland: ISO, 2015a.

ISO (International Organization for Standardization). ISO 12647-7, *Graphic Technology—Proofing Processes Working Directly from Digital Data*. Geneva, Switzerland: ISO, 2015b.

ISO/PAS (International Organization for Standardization). ISO/PAS 15339-1, *Graphic Technology—Printing from Digital Data across Multiple Technologies*. Part 1, *Principles*. Geneva, Switzerland: ISO, 2015c.

ISO/PAS (International Organization for Standardization). ISO/PAS 15339-2, *Graphic Technology—Printing from Digital Data across Multiple Technologies*. Part 2, *Characterized Reference Printing Conditions*. Geneva, Switzerland: ISO, 2015d.

ISO (International Organization for Standardization). ISO/TR 19300.4, *Graphic Technology—Guidelines for the Use of Standards for Print Media Production Workflows*. Geneva, Switzerland: ISO, 2015e.

ISO (International Organization for Standardization). ISO 20654, *Graphic Technology—Measurement and Calculation of Spot Color Tonal Value*. Geneva, Switzerland: ISO, 2016.

ISO (International Organization for Standardization). ISO 19301, *Graphic Technology—Guidelines for Schema Writers—Template for Colour Quality Management*. Geneva, Switzerland: ISO, 2017a.

ISO (International Organization for Standardization). ISO 19302, *Graphic Technology—Colour Conformity of Printed Products*. Geneva, Switzerland: ISO, 2017b.

ISO (International Organization for Standardization). ISO/TS 19303-1, *Graphic Technology—Certification Scheme Guidelines*. Part 1, *Packaging Printing*. Geneva, Switzerland: ISO, 2017c.

ISO (International Organization for Standardization). ISO/TS 15311-1, *Graphic Technology—Print Quality Requirements for Printed Matter*. Part 1, *Measurement Methods and Reporting Schema*. Geneva, Switzerland: ISO, 2018a.

ISO (International Organization for Standardization). ISO/PDTS 18621-31.4, *Graphic Technology—Image Quality Evaluation Methods for Printed Matter Utilizing Digital Printing Technologies in Commercial and Industrial Production*. Part 31, *Evaluation of the Perceived Resolution of Printing Systems with the Contrast-Resolution Chart*. Geneva, Switzerland: ISO, 2018b.

Luke, Joy. *The Munsell Color System, A Language for Color*. New York: Fairchild Publications, 1996.

MacCurtain, Sean. "Conformity Assessment and the CASCO Toolbox." Paper presented at ISO/TC 130 meeting, Berlin, Germany, September 16, 2011.

McDowell, David. "US Involvement in Graphic Arts Standards Activity—A Partial History." *TAGA Proceedings* 1996: 235–253.

McDowell, David. "Graphic Arts Color Standards." *TAGA Proceedings* 1999: 661–671.

McDowell, David, Robert Chung, and Lingjun Kong. "Correcting Measured Colorimetric Data for Differences in Backing Material." *TAGA Proceedings* 2005: 302–310.

McDowell, David. "The Transformation of Backing Correction to Substrate Correction." *TAGA Proceedings* 2012: 268–282.

Murray, Alexander, "Monochrome Reproduction in Photoengraving," *Journal of the Franklin Institute*, vol. 221, no. 6 (1936): 721–744.

Myers, Bruce, Sanyukta Hiremath, David Pflantz, Victoria Wildow, Tommy Hodgson, Alexander Greenhalgh, Nuanjan Narakornpijit, and Chandramohan Srinivasaraju, *Test Targets 11.0*, Rochester, NY: RIT School of Media Sciences, 2018.

Rickmers, Albert, and Hollis Todd. *Statistics, An Introduction*. New York: McGraw-Hill, 1967.

Sharma, Abhay. *Understanding Color Management*. 2nd ed. Hoboken, NJ: Wiley, 2018.

Tollenaar, D., and, P. A. H. Ernst. "Optical Density and Ink Layer Thickness: Problems in High Speed Printing." *IARIGAI Proceedings*. Oxford, UK: Pergamon Press, 1962.

Wheeler, Donald. *Understanding Variation, the Key to Managing Chaos*. Knoxville, TN: SPC Press, 1993.

Index

Colophon

Editor
Molly Q. Cort

Designer
Marnie Soom

Printer
More Vang
Alexandria, Virginia

Paper
100 lb. Blazer Silk cover, 80 lb. Blazer Silk text

Typefaces
Palatino Linotype
Neue Haas Grotesk

This book was made possible, in part, through the generosity of
John Williams and More Vang.